MAKE ROOM FOR GOD

MAKE ROOM FOR GOD
clearing out the clutter

SUSAN K. ROWLAND

ST. ANTHONY MESSENGER PRESS
Cincinnati, Ohio

Scripture passages have been taken from *New Revised Standard Version Bible,* copyright ©1989 by the Division of Christian Education of the National Council of the Churches of Christ in the U.S.A., and used by permission. All rights reserved.

Cover design by Sandy L. Digman
Cover image © iStockphoto.com/Chris Riccio
Book design by Mark Sullivan

LIBRARY OF CONGRESS CATALOGING-IN-PUBLICATION DATA

Rowland, Susan K.
Make room for God : clearing out the clutter / Susan K. Rowland.
p. cm.
Includes bibliographical references.
ISBN-13: 978-0-86716-778-8 (pbk. : alk. paper)
ISBN-10: 0-86716-778-5 (pbk. : alk. paper) 1. Spiritual life—Catholic Church. 2. Simplicity—Religious aspects—Catholic Church. 3. Time management—Religious aspects—Christianity. I. Title.

BX2350.3.R68 2007
248.4—dc22

2006037306

ISBN 978-0-86716-778-8

Published by St. Anthony Messenger Press
28 W. Liberty St.
Cincinnati, OH 45202
www.AmericanCatholic.org

Printed in the United States of America.

Printed on acid-free paper.

07 08 09 10 5 4 3 2

To my sons, Tony, Matt and Mike

ACKNOWLEDGMENTS

Thank you: Lisa Biedenbach, Mary Hackett and the staff of St. Anthony Messenger Press; Fr. Tom Santa, Charles Roth and everyone at the Catholic Writers' Retreats in Tucson, Arizona; Monsignor Lou Gaetano, who insisted that I was put here on earth not to *do* things, but to *become* someone; the Reverend Marian Fortner of All Saints Episcopal Church, Phoenix, for ideas in the worry chapter; Dr. Joe Torma of Walsh University in North Canton, Ohio, especially for his thoughts on prayer; Rabbi John Spitzer, also of Walsh University, for teaching me about the Sabbath; Barbara Georgescu, for teaching me about community; Jan Parisian, my first reader, for her wise suggestions and most of the chapter activities; my mother, Ida Bielecki, my brother Thom Spring, and my friend, Marilyn Collins, for their support, encouragement and advice; members of the adult education classes and Single Parents' group at St. George Parish, Apache Junction, Arizona, for letting me try out this material on them and for offering their suggestions; and all the members of my parish family at St. Timothy's in Mesa, Arizona, especially the Women's Fellowship, for your friendship and for loving the Lord and not being afraid to express that love. Finally, thank you Spencer and Kelsey for providing me joy and laughter and great stories to share.

CONTENTS

INTRODUCTION

Lost in the Wilderness: A Parable

I live in a little neighborhood at the base of the Superstition Mountains east of Phoenix. The views of the mountain on one side and the city lights on the other, the beauty of the Sonoran Desert and even the coyotes, javelina and bobcats who wander the streets make living here an adventure, especially for a girl born in New York City. A half-mile from my front door is the Superstition Wilderness of Tonto National Forest.

Recently, my dog and I were taking our usual late-afternoon walk and decided to leave the paved road and head into the wilderness. We would go just a short way; I had no water or flashlight. But there was plenty of time for a quick walk before sundown.

Kelsey led the way, following a path I could barely see. She knew exactly where to go by following the scents of the wild animals and horses that use this trail. We came to a flat boulder, a rarity in these parts. After checking for stray rattlesnakes, scorpions and cactus thorns, we sat down to enjoy the view. The rock was hard, but Kelsey sat on my leg and made herself comfortable. I closed my eyes and let the silence of the desert envelop me.

After what seemed a very short time, I opened my eyes and looked to the west. The sun was much lower than it should have been. No matter. We had only walked into the wilderness for about ten minutes, and I could see the houses and water tower nearby. "Let's go," I told the dog as I pushed her off me. Kelsey picked up the path again and trotted confidently ahead.

It wasn't long before I realized something was wrong. We were still walking the same path, but landmarks that had been ahead of us earlier were now behind us. The mountain was getting closer and the neighborhood farther away. I stopped and began to feel a tiny bit of panic. "We have to go *home*, Kelsey," I said. "Let's go *home*."

Kelsey smiled and seemed to say, "Okay. Gotcha." She made a U-turn and headed back the way we had come. Like me, Kelsey is a city girl, so her show of confidence didn't impress me. Suspecting she was as lost as I was, I began to pray and to look for the side path we must have missed. I finally saw it, a faint line perpendicular to the path we were on. Going in, I had not realized we had turned onto a new path. The entrance to it on the other side was obscured by bushes grown lush and green during recent rains. Kelsey marched right by it again.

Breathing a sigh of relief, I called the dog back and turned toward home, and then muttered to myself that someone needed to mark the turnoff with some bright orange paint. Soon we began to see familiar landmarks and then the gate at the trailhead. We made it home just as the sun set.

Night is not a good time to be out alone in the desert.

This was not the first time I had been lost in a wilderness.

Not long ago, I was wandering around in my own little world, stressed out by all the things I believed I had to do, frustrated by the clutter that was filling my closets and my mind, and all the while longing for something better. I worked too much, prayed too little and added to my load with long lists that never got done. I read books on time management and simplicity and implemented their suggestions, but my life stayed the same.

Sound familiar? If so, you are normal. This is what our culture expects of us: work, work and more work; do, do and more doing. "What do you do?" is what we ask when introduced. "Keep your nose to the grindstone" is considered wisdom. "I'll rest when I'm dead" is a bumper sticker and a praiseworthy attitude.

In 2000 my life moved from frustrating to impossible. That was the year my husband of thirty years announced he wanted a divorce. To make matters even worse, our three sons were ready to leave for college, and I was going to be left in an empty nest.

I began to spiral into a deep depression. All my buried fears of abandonment and failure came to the surface. For years I had barricaded them by doing and buying, worrying and putting off my own dreams to make sure everyone around me was okay. My life, the proverbial house of cards, was collapsing under the clutter of my life.

It was obvious I would either have a nervous breakdown or have to learn a new way to live. I decided to learn a new way to live. With God's guidance and the help of dear friends, a great spiritual director and a patient Christian psychologist, I learned God's perspective about the meaning of life. Guided by the principle it is more important to *be* than it is to *do*, I made big changes in how I was living my life, one tiny step at a time. Over the next few years I found, to my joy and amazement, God did not want me to live the way I had been living my life. God knows the way out of the wilderness and how to bring us home.

During my journey I read many self-help books. Stores are full of books with suggestions and techniques on how to deal with life today. There are books on simplicity, organization, productivity and efficiency, to name just a few. Although a few were helpful, none seemed to work for me because none penetrated my unique issues deep enough—no one book seemed to speak to me as a person of faith.

This book does not promote yet another method or technique. Instead, *Make Room for God: Clearing Out the Clutter* affords one an attitude adjustment, or more aptly, a new set of glasses with which to view life. It is the result of praying, learning new lessons and unlearning old ones. It includes input from real people—family, friends and participants in my parish adult education classes—whose lives are also stressful, cluttered and unfocused. The principles in this book work because they allow each of us to make the changes we need to make, one change at a time, and most importantly, when we feel ready to make these changes.

Read this book with an open heart. It is a record of my life's lessons that have ultimately shown me what is important to God and me, and what has and has not worked previously for me. These are the lessons God taught me in my real and cluttered life, which is probably much like yours. Using these principles, you will find as I did that you can live a simpler, freer, less cluttered life. You can manage your work and have better relationships with God and other people. You can even find time and permission to follow your creative impulses, the sure mark of the Creator in you.

If you feel lost in our cultural wilderness, in clutter, collecting, consuming, working, worrying and waiting for something better, I wrote this book for you. I have been lost, too. God has shown me a way out. This book is a bit of bright orange paint pointing toward the path home.

Let's walk it together.

How To Use This Book

I have arranged this book to cover the basic aspects of living an uncluttered life first, then moving into deeper spiritual work. These lessons include caring for our bodies, clearing out our homes, working well, waiting for God, forgiving others, praying regularly, keeping the Sabbath, living in community and allowing our creative natures to shine. All are part of *Make Room for God: Clearing Out the Clutter.*

1. Be patient and trust God.

As you work through this book, be patient with yourself and trust God. It took us a long time to get to this point in our secular culture; it took each of us our whole lives to get where we are today. We need to give ourselves time to learn new ways of living. We have time, but only if we begin now.

2. Read through the entire book before making any decisions.

I recommend reading this entire book through the first time without doing any projects or even making decisions about where to start. However, you may begin your good-morning journal (see chapter two), play the evacuation game (explained in detail in chapter four) and make the suggested lists that you will find in chapters eight, seventeen and nineteen during the first reading.

After reading the book at least once, you will have a good idea of which areas you want to work on first. You will be excited about starting and hopeful about the results.

3. Reread the sections that interest you.
Do the activities for those chapters, and study them well before implementing the suggestions.

4. Get help.
Find a good friend to help you declutter, a prayer partner or group that will pray with you, perhaps a counselor to help you through difficult forgiveness issues.

5. Pace yourself.
Do not be overwhelmed if there are multiple areas of your life needing attention. I have worked through every one of these issues over the last few years. Deal with one task at a time. You do not have to do it all now; you cannot do it all now. Don't try! Today, I feel great about my life, but it took time and patience. I now work better, and my house is neat most of the time. But I still have to control new piles of paper. Old forgiveness issues resurface. I can forget to spend time with God.

6. Remember: Strive for improvement, not perfection.
Life is like that. We will never have every aspect of our lives under control; nothing will ever be perfect. What we are striving for is improvement. We want to move toward peace, order and the freedom to be who we are meant to be.

7. Revisit the book, monthly, biannually or annually or whatever works for your schedule.
This book is meant to help you over the years. Work on one, at the most two, areas at a time. When you feel one area is improved, move gently onto the next.

SECTION ONE

SELF-CARE WITHOUT CLUTTER

In this section we consider some of our basic human needs. The first is to examine what we believe about ourselves, about God and about our culture's demands on us. Are these demands the same as God's?

Then we learn a new and simple way to start each day centered on God. We also discuss the basics of taking care of our bodies.

These are the first steps to living an uncluttered spiritual life. We must examine our expectations and beliefs. We must pray. And we must take care of our bodies.

CHAPTER ONE

"I SHOULD BE DOING BETTER!"

> We have bought the message of our culture: this world is a
> vale of tears and we are meant to be dutiful and then die.
> —Julia Cameron, *The Artist's Way: A Spiritual Path to Creativity*[1]

HOW ARE YOU?

Seriously, how are you?

I don't mean now, as you are reading this book. I mean your life in general. How is it going?

I teach adult education classes at my church. Recently, I asked this question of a group of parents. Their answers were painful: "I'm too busy." "Life is chaotic." "My life is confusing." "I'm very forgetful." "I'm angry a lot." "I have low self-esteem." "There is never enough time." "I should be doing better."

The last comment was the most revealing. Why should the young mother who said this be doing better? Because everyone else is?

MAKE ROOM FOR GOD

This could be the rallying cry of our society today: "I should be doing better. Everyone *else* seems to be okay. Why don't *I* feel okay?"

Our culture—meaning early twenty-first-century western culture—places some unfair demands on us. Most cultures throughout history have done the same, but we don't live then. We live now. So let us examine our culture's demands. Do they coincide with what our faith tells us? Are they interfering with the fulfillment of the promises of our faith? This is a book about living a spiritual life in our culture, so these are vital questions.

I believe our western (American) culture keeps us from developing spiritually and becoming the people God created us to be.

This is not surprising. We live in a fallen world. Our particular culture seems to worship the god of productivity. It is isolationist and consumerist. Many of us neglect God and other relationships while we work excessively to fulfill temporal needs like buying a home and paying for our children's education and our retirement. Do we think we will then attend to the spiritual side of life?

Life does not work that way. Jesus warned us about losing our souls to gain the world (Matthew 16:26). We will not suddenly develop into spiritual beings with real values when we retire or when we reach some pinnacle of success. Spirituality is not a function of a paid-off mortgage, a desired promotion or a hefty retirement account. Those are all earthly goals; they are secondary to preparing for eternity. If we are wise enough to prepare for the day when we can no longer work, why do we not prepare for the day when we leave this world? We know our earthly lives are going to end. Our spiritual needs must not be put off until "someday."

Many of us, myself included at one time, think we will

"become spiritual" when our lives settle down or when we reach a certain goal. This is a fallacy. Things never settle down. The goal reached or the stressful event or season is always replaced by another urgent goal or project.

For a long time, I felt like a failure because my life and home were hopelessly cluttered. I could not keep up with the work. I never got to the end of my to-do lists. Worst of all, I believed a whole set of cultural tenets: *Good people get a lot done. God expects us to work hard in this life. Everyone else is doing fine, and I am not if I can't do what they are doing.* These beliefs are actually part of our cultural "religion," which many of us accept unquestioningly and unconsciously. They are not true, and they are not part of our Christian faith.

Julia Cameron, author of *The Artist's Way*, put it best when she wrote, "[W]e have bought the message of our culture: this world is a vale of tears and we are meant to be dutiful and then die."[2] Many of us think this philosophy is spiritual. We think that is all there is to this life: to be dutiful and die, to suffer to earn eternity.

When dutifully doing things becomes the focus of our lives, we will never fulfill God's true purpose for us or our deepest longings. We will never come to the end of our to-do lists. The world will never excuse us from one task or duty. We will never get to the really important things in life unless we intentionally carve out time for them. Our essential selves, our purpose in life, our relationships with God and other people have too long been put aside and belittled by this culture that worships accomplishment.

God has a much better plan for us than working and suffering all our lives. "Doing" does not equal worthiness or holiness. God does not expect us to spend this life working to the point of exhaustion and putting relationships and creativity aside in favor of getting just one more task done. God has other dreams for us.

WHO ARE YOU BECOMING?

We were not created by God to *do* things! We were created to *be* someone. God does not need us to do things. God is perfectly capable of doing anything that needs to be done. We are not worker bees in some cosmic hive, beasts of burden or slaves. We were created to be like God, to become sons and daughters, beloved children of God.

The last section of this book is entitled "Practicing for Eternity," which is what we are doing as human beings, whether we realize it or not.

God created us to live forever. This life is only Phase One, the first, awkward steps an infant takes in a protected, baby-gated environment before going out into the world, where the real learning happens. In a sense, our time on earth is a spiritual kindergarten. We are meant to use this life to learn who we are, who our Creator is and where we fit into the eternal design.

The first lesson we as people of faith must learn is this: *Doing* things is not nearly as important as *becoming* who we are meant to be. If all God wanted was for us to do things, we would be machines. God wants us to become someone.

Doing is part of our calling. It flows from and expresses our being. But our culture emphasizes *doing* so much—in the form of that greatest of virtues: productivity—we are in real danger of forgetting who we *are*.

How do we know we are forgetting who we are? We are forgetting who we are when:

- we think that being productive and getting things done are what God expects.

- we go from task to task, obligation to obligation, all the while thinking we will be "done" someday and then we can start living.

- we rush through each day, doing only what the next crisis demands, and fall into bed exhausted, only to wake up and repeat the cycle again.
- we have a vague, uncomfortable feeling that we are neglecting our relationships, including the one with God.

When we forget who we really are, we miss out on the most important things in life: joy, peace, serenity and even love.

NOTE
[1] Julia Cameron, *The Artist's Way: A Spiritual Path to Higher Creativity* (New York: Putnam, 1992), p. 194.
[2] Cameron, p. 194.

CHAPTER TWO

THE FIRST TASK: REMEMBERING

[T]he real problem of the Christian life comes…the very
moment you wake up each morning. All your wishes and
hopes for the day rush at you like wild animals. And the first
job each morning consists simply in shoving them all back;
in listening to that other voice, taking that other point of
view, letting that other larger, stronger, quieter life
come flowing in.—C.S. Lewis, *Mere Christianity*[1]

My very favorite movie of 2004, maybe my all-time favorite, was
50 First Dates, starring Drew Barrymore and Adam Sandler. In
this sweet love story, Barrymore's character, Lucy, suffers from a
rare form of amnesia caused by a head injury. Each day's memories are erased during the night as she sleeps. She wakes up every
morning believing it is the morning of her accident.

I watched this movie over and over, fascinated by Lucy's
boyfriend, who must introduce himself to her every day and
work to make her fall in love with him daily. This movie offers

an important lesson, which we as spiritual people should learn. Lucy must wake up each day, catch up with what has happened in her life since her accident and get back into step with reality. In other words, she has to remember who she is. Lucy uses a videotape and a daily journal (both labeled "Good Morning, Lucy") to help her. Her amnesia never goes away, but she marries her true love and has a family, in spite of the daily struggle with her damaged brain.

We are all Lucy, except we have amnesia of the spirit. We begin each day in groggy confusion, immediately rushing to start the day's tasks: kids, spouse, getting ready for school and work, making breakfast, thinking about the day's tasks, rushing to appointments.

I know a few people who begin their days by waking earlier than the rest of the family and devoting the first half-hour of the day to prayer. For me, and most of the people I talk to, our waking routine is quite the opposite. We begin by forgetting.

I decided to begin my day the way Lucy does in *50 First Dates*, by keeping a "Good Morning, Susan" journal of simple truths about me and about God. Coming up with the journal was not easy at first, but I began with a message my friend Marilyn has taped to her clock radio. It says, in essence, "This is God. I will be handling all your troubles today, so have a nice day."

This led to deeper messages, letters from God telling me how much he loves me. There were little bits of advice on staying centered and reminders about my true identity as God's daughter. There was nothing about getting through my to-do lists. When I faithfully read my good-morning journal, it centers me, reminds me of my identity and keeps me from rushing off to do things, all the while forgetting about God.

CREATING YOUR OWN GOOD-MORNING JOURNAL

First, get yourself a small, blank journal. Start with writing in anything you have on hand, but I recommend finding something you really like.

Keep in mind the good-morning journal is not the daily writing journal many of us keep. The good-morning journal is for recording the special things that remind us of our deepest selves, of what we know about God and of what we know to be true. It may have excerpts from our other journals, Scripture passages and book quotations. It is for lessons we have learned in life that are true, no matter what our circumstances. If you still have no idea where to start, write out Psalm 139:1–18.

If you are already a regular journal writer, look through your journals for favorite passages. These are very important nuggets of information and insights into your true self and your relationship with God over the years. Copy them into your good-morning journal.

The good-morning journal will evolve over time. Do not be afraid to rip the whole thing up and start over completely. Your good-morning journal must reflect who you are right now. As you get deeper and deeper into your spirituality, expect the journal to change. More than anything, trust yourself to know what belongs in your journal.

After putting time and effort into making our good-morning journals, we should remember to read them—every morning before we start our day. Though this journal idea is my brainchild, I often forget to read my own—a classic example of "do as I say, not as I do." I have propped my journal against my clock radio and placed it in other conspicuous spots, yet still I forget to read it or find excuses why I don't have the time to do so.

Don't get discouraged if you are forgetful, or that you can't seem to make time to read it. All new habits take time to form.

When the benefits and calm of this daily practice begin to manifest themselves, you will remember. It is like using the seat belt in your car. After years of buckling up, I feel naked without my seat belt. I now feel a strange emptiness when I don't read my good-morning journal.

One of my adult students asked me what to do if he oversleeps in the morning. Once the good-morning journal is set up, it will take only a few minutes to read. You are already late. Take those few minutes to center on God so the day, which may have begun inauspiciously, will not become totally rotten!

Don't worry if you cannot think clearly first thing in the morning. The messages in the journal should be easy to absorb and understand. After all, they are thoughts and messages that you have already connected with on some level. This should not be complex reading. For example, the messages I have written in my journal are simple truths: God loves you. You are a worthy person. You are God's child. And the more you read your journal and get in the habit of doing so, it will ultimately change your outlook on life, even if you are half-asleep when you read it.

Ask the Holy Spirit to help you when developing and using your good-morning journal. Did you know that "reminding" is one of the Holy Spirit's jobs (see John 14:27)? This is also a great passage to copy into your journal.

Write in your journal at any time. Some people work on them first thing in the morning, but that will not work for those already late for work. Choose a good time for you, when it is quiet and you are able to listen to God, read Scripture or other special resources which contain positive, life-affirming messages and truths—such as your old journals, letters, favorite books, poetry or songs.

In his book *Keep It Simple: The Busy Catholic's Guide to Growing Closer to God*, the late French bishop Emmanuel de

Gibergues, told the story of a hermit who always paused and looked toward the heavens before he did anything. Asked why, the hermit said, "The better to make sure of my aim."[2]

The good-morning journal is a great way to "take aim" at the beginning of your day. You may even find yourself keeping it in your purse or briefcase to glance at throughout the day to continue "taking aim" wherever you are. This is not the only praying we should be doing, but it's a start.

NOTES

[1] C.S. Lewis, *Mere Christianity* (New York: MacMillan, 1960), pp. 168–169.

[2] Emmanuel de Gibergues, *Keep It Simple: The Busy Catholic's Guide to Growing Closer to God* (Manchester, N.H.: Sophia Institute, 2000), p. 88.

CHAPTER THREE

TAKING CARE OF THE BASICS

It is in vain that you rise up early
and go late to rest,
eating the bread of anxious toil;
for [the Lord] gives sleep to his beloved.
—Psalm 127:2

EATING, DRINKING, SLEEPING AND TAKING CARE OF OURSELVES

Why, in a spirituality book of all things, are we going to discuss physical health? Why am I, who *am* is not an expert in medical science, going to discuss the importance of taking care of the body? Because, we all, myself included, need to stop, listen and learn all over again, how to take care of ourselves before we take care of anyone else.

Several years ago I taught the lessons in this chapter as part of a lenten adult education series. To my surprise, people pulled out paper, took copious notes and asked me a lot of questions. Many of us do not think much about taking care of our bodies. We are so busy being productive and doing "stuff" for everyone else, we need to learn again how to care for ourselves.

Any discussion of spirituality, of right living, even of God's will for us, has to start with taking care of the bodies God gave us. We are incarnate spirits, which means we express ourselves through our physical bodies. Even in eternity, we will have physical bodies. These new bodies will work better and will never die, but they will be physical. The body is not a shell, like a piece of clothing that we can abuse, ignore, take off and throw away. If we neglect our bodies, our minds and spirits will suffer and be unable to express our being. Have you ever noticed how hard it is to be kind, patient and aware of God when you are hungry, thirsty, sleep-deprived and tense?

We express our beings through doing, but we do everything through the body as our instrument. So we must keep our bodies well-nourished, hydrated and rested. If we do, our bodies will serve us well.

THE MANY WAYS WE ABUSE OURSELVES

Karen Scalf Linamen, author of *Just Hand Over the Chocolate and No One Will Get Hurt*, lists a few: nipple piercing, bungee jumping, bikini waxes and watching the Star Trek Marathon on the Sci-Fi Channel until 3:00 AM.

People today, myself included, seem to prefer the classic abuses: eating unhealthily, drinking very little water and forcing ourselves to function all day on little or no sleep. And we seldom allow ourselves to relax. (Collapsing in front of the television in the evening does not count!)

We Eat Too Much

Let's start with food. Americans today are the heaviest they have ever been, in spite of the health food and exercise movements of the last few decades. Though the topic is not the focus of this book, it cannot be ignored. And believe me it's hard to ignore it. Everywhere we look it's obvious: Americans, especially, are "filling up" on all the wrong things. The busy-ness of our lives has pushed us through fast food drive-thrus or dinners in front of the television instead of around the kitchen table with family or friends—and it has pushed us right into obesity. We're a lonely, "hungry" society that is self-medicating with unhealthy foods. In our cyclical or seasonal crash diets, we try to deny ourselves, only to fall back into our old habits when things don't go as planned or we don't lose the weight we had hoped to. But there is a way out of this cycle if you just stop and listen to what your body is saying, not to mention some good (non-fad) medical people:

- Eat three well-balanced, portion-controlled meals and several small, healthy snacks throughout the day.
- Eat from a variety of foods and lots of vegetable matter.
- Don't eat packaged foods full of salt, preservatives and flavor enhancers.
- Don't deny yourself the foods that you truly enjoy; rather, eat them in moderation.
- Remind yourself daily that the only diet that works is the one you can use for the rest of your life.

We Don't Drink Enough Water

The second way we abuse ourselves is dehydration. With the advent of the extreme marketing of soft drinks and sports drinks, most of us are not drinking enough plain water. I live in the desert where the average humidity is about 12 percent. We desert dwellers soon learn the importance of drinking lots of water. If we do not drink water, we feel lousy and watch our skin shrivel. Water is just as necessary in nondesert areas. Americans are chronically dehydrated, partially because of our unhealthy diets and partially because of all the stress that is part of our lifestyles.

Though science and research has confirmed the importance of staying hydrated, anecdotally I can confirm what the scientists already figured out. During my last job I had a terrible time focusing after lunch, no matter how little I ate. I thought this was a normal afternoon slump. Then, I started drinking a large glass of water after I ate, and I sipped more water all afternoon. The results were nearly miraculous. I stayed wide awake and ready to work all afternoon. Now I keep water with me on my desk whenever I am writing. If I feel a slump coming on, I drink some water and it helps me to focus the rest of the day.

We Don't Sleep Enough

Let's consider our sleep habits, another area of physical health we neglect. Many of us need much more sleep than we are getting. According to the National Sleep Foundation's 2005 Sleep in America poll, 52 percent of those surveyed felt they were not getting enough sleep. So, how much sleep is enough? While scientists differ (slightly) in stating how much sleep we need, the consensus seems to be somewhere between seven and nine hours per night, far more than most busy Americans get. I know that I was trying to get along on six hours or less (statistically, I was three times more likely to have a "drowsy driving" car crash). I now have upped my nighttime sleep allotment to eight hours, and I am feeling much better. In spite of everything our culture demands of us, until science can change our biology, we had better stick to this basic.

Here are a few helpful hints from the experts about how to get more sleep:

• Work your way up to eight hours if you are getting a lot less.
• Remove all electronics from the bedroom.
• A moderately boring book, not television, is the best sleep aid.

- Never, never lie down in front of the television and allow yourself to fall asleep in the evening.
- Force yourself to turn off the TV and get to bed by a certain time, even if you have to set an alarm to make yourself get up and go to bed.

Helpful Hints to Help You Sleep
- When you are ready to go to sleep, pause for a moment to reflect on your day.
- If possible, step outside and look up at the night sky or look up at the sky through a window from a darkened room.
- Calm and relax yourself by telling yourself that God is watching over you. Keep the same level of calm as you climb into bed. If you are anxious about something you have to do tomorrow, write it down, commit the matter to God's care and forget it.

If none of these things work and you have a constant problem sleeping, you might want to go to a sleep center and be tested. Chronic insomnia is not normal—the body God gave you is designed to sleep. If you cannot sleep, it is often a sign of a treatable medical condition.

We Don't Relax
Another way we abuse our bodies is by never allowing ourselves to relax. Many of us use television to unwind, but watching TV is not really relaxing. The electronic signals, loud advertisements and usual programming are not designed for that. In fact, a lot of the news, talk shows and so-called reality shows seem intended to make us excited and even angry. After a hard day we may look forward to hours of mind-numbing sitcoms, sports or drama, especially with large quantities of snack foods. This is not relaxing, and it's not good for our bodies. Wouldn't it be better to work on a hobby you love (gardening, crafts, whatever), turn on some soft music, read a good book or play with the kids or pets?

Try this experiment: Do your usual TV watching in the evening for a week; then try a week doing something totally different. During both weeks keep track of how you feel during the day. Are you more or less stressed? Did you get more or less work done? If there is a noticeable difference, you have some decisions to make.

Most of us do not know how to breathe. To relax throughout the day, especially when you are getting stressed, learn to breathe deeply. Start by closing your eyes and breathing out through your mouth while sucking in your lower abdomen. Now, let go. Let your whole lower abdomen drop. My singing coach said it should feel like a sudden "clunk." You will notice your lungs fill without your having to pull any air in. You are releasing your diaphragm and making room for your lungs to expand. They will automatically. Repeat this technique slowly for five minutes.

What this little exercise does—besides filling up our lungs with nice oxygen—is cut stress levels to almost nothing. "Take a deep breath" is good advice in a lot of circumstances. It is one biological function we can control at will, but most of us don't know how. Practice that releasing mechanism. Use it throughout the day. It releases tension, calms us down and wakes us up. And it's free. What more could anyone want?

ACTIVITIES

1. Make an inventory of your habits regarding food, water and sleep. Are you satisfied with your level of self-care in these areas? What improvements might you make?

2. Imagine your life without television or very limited hours of television. How would life be different? What would you do instead?

3. Practice the deep-breathing technique. Use it in a stressful situation when you feel yourself getting angry, tense or overwhelmed. What happened?

SECTION TWO

AN ENVIRONMENT WITHOUT CLUTTER

How cluttered is your environment? Is your home jam-packed with furniture, knickknacks, appliances, electronics and gadgets? Is every closet and drawer stuffed with odd papers, old bills, faded receipts, magazines, broken toys, outdated clothes, loose marbles and other mysterious objects that you don't even know how they got there in the first place? Does clutter overflow every surface? Do you lose things regularly? Do you feel lost?

The purpose of this section is to understand that physical clutter interferes with our well-being, and thus with our spiritual lives.

First, we play a game that reveals our true attitude toward our possessions. We explore some of the reasons we collect so many things. In the last two chapters we learn practical ways to get our messes under control, learning how to clear out our physical surroundings, then our paper clutter.

CHAPTER FOUR

What *Is* All This Stuff?

The more we simplify our material life,
the more time we will have to live.
—T. Alexander Anderson, *The Gift of Time: Making the Most
of Your Time and Your Life*[1]

We have examined our cultural attitudes, learned about a new
tool (the good-morning journal) to help us center ourselves at
the beginning of each day and looked at how well or badly we
are taking care of our bodies. This is only a beginning.

Now let's look around at our physical surroundings. Like
most people, our homes and offices get a tiny bit out of control
and frustrating, don't they?

This section is all about bringing order to our chaos, reduc-
ing clutter, thus making our surroundings less stressful. Our
homes, especially, should be where we go at the end of a stressful day, where we can be peaceful and relaxed, where we are surrounded by loved ones and belongings which enhance our lives.

We will start by playing a game. Do not skip this step; it is
important. It's also a lot of fun.

THE EVACUATION GAME
(or "You can take it with you!")

A very nice angel has knocked on your door and announced we are all evacuating. God is shutting down the planet and relocating us to a nicer one. We will never return, but all our basic needs will be supplied on the new planet: home, food, cooking utensils, clothes and toiletries.

Children and pets are, of course, included in the evacuation.

Best of all, we may take anything material with us we want. God understands we all have things we really like, things that express who we are.

Size is not an issue. Each member of the family is given a large bag and a magic wand with which to shrink anything too large to go into the bag.

There is one wrinkle in this plan: We only have three minutes to go through our home and decide what we will be taking.

The Rules

1. You may not spend more than thirty seconds in any room. Move through your house in any order you choose, but you may only visit a room once and only for thirty seconds. If you have too many rooms in your house, you have to skip some or get through more than one in a thirty-second period (or if you have less rooms, divide the three minutes up accordingly).

2. Use pencil and paper in lieu of a magic wand to write down items you want to take.

3. Use a clock or watch with a second hand to keep track of the six thirty-second periods. One person may be designated the timekeeper for the rest of the family or group. He or she then takes a turn "gathering" while another person keeps time. No one gets to do this exercise again if they forgot something important.

4. Younger children may play this game with the help of a parent. In fact, it is a very good idea to let your children play, even if they are preschoolers. Give your child a "magic wand" and have her touch things she wants while you write down the item. Make sure to tell him this is pretend or he will be looking for angels at the door and packing his little bag!

5. Play the game in two ways: Do it first in your imagination, mentally walking through the house and remembering where things are. Next, do it while actually walking through your house. This is very revealing.

When you are finished with the Evacuation Game, immediately assess the results. Here are some questions to guide you:

1. Was there a big difference between what you "saved" when you did the game mentally and when you walked through your house and actually looked at each room? Why?

2. Were you surprised at what you did "save" and what you let go?

3. Were your spouse's and children's choices surprising?

4. Were there any rooms where *nothing* was saved by any family member? Was this surprising?

5. What would your current house look like if it were only furnished with the essentials (like basic cookware and clothing) plus the things you "saved" during the game?

6. Were there things you would have "saved" but you forgot about them until later or until another family member mentioned them? Are there important things in your house so obscured by other items you didn't remember they were there?

7. Were there things you left deliberately? Things you would be relieved to be rid of if only such a scenario presented itself? ("Sorry, mom, but we didn't have room for the six-foot bunny you knitted for us.")

8. Honestly, do you have too many things?

9. If you discuss the game with your spouse and children, keep in mind some family members' choices may seem peculiar or even hilarious. Hopefully, there will be a lot of laughter as family members share their lists. Please remember to be respectful of each person's choices. The things we love express who we are right now. Nothing is "stupid." Knowing how other family members feel about the things in your home will help you know them better and make a good discussion-starter.

Things change in life. We all get older and have different priorities. The Evacuation Game is a fun way to reassess what we are keeping and why. Something precious to us today may not be important in a few years. It's okay to get rid of those things and make room for something else. It is also okay to love our things. They express who we are in some way.

ACTIVITY

Keep your Evacuation list by your side as you continue reading. You may add anything important you forgot but keep the list "as is" unless the forgotten items are very important to you. We are going to discuss sorting, decluttering and making our homes beautiful, less stressful places. Our lists show us which of our possessions are really important to us and which mean very little to us.

Note
[1] T. Alexander Anderson, *The Gift of Time: Making the Most of Your Time and Your Life* (Edina, Minn.: TMPress, 2001), p. 75.

CHAPTER FIVE

WHY WE COLLECT—AND WHAT IT COSTS US

Our lives are shaky, contingent, uncertain, fragile affairs....
Therefore we try to build up for ourselves a base
which would be at least temporarily secure and from
which we could defend ourselves and fight
off the rest of the world.
—Andrew M. Greeley, *When Life Hurts: Healing Themes from the
Gospels*[1]

We once had a dog named Spencer, a very pretty Dalmatian. When we got him at four months old, we read enough of the Dr. Spock-ish doggie books to know Spencer needed his own kennel to be properly housetrained and to have his own private place to go to for naps and meditation, or whatever it is dogs do. We built him a kennel in our basement, and he adjusted very well. He never cried at night after the first few nights, and he often went into his "hidey hole" during the day to nap and relax.

A few weeks after Spencer's arrival, I had the following conversation, in various forms, with all three of my sons:

"Mom, where is my favorite red shirt?"

"I don't know. Where *is* your favorite red shirt?"

"I can't find it anywhere. Have you done the laundry lately?" (Meaning, "in the last six months").

"Yes, I've done all the laundry. Did you look around your room, like under the bed?"

"Yes, I've looked everywhere. Where could it be? I wanted to wear it today."

This conversation, repeated several times, became a little annoying. So I looked under beds, around the laundry room, even under the furniture in the family room. Everyone seemed to be missing favorite articles of clothing, even me. Standing in the middle of the basement, scratching my head, I happened to glance into Spencer's kennel. There was a pile of material in there, more than the old blankets we had given him. Some of it was red, much of it looked suspiciously like human clothing. You guessed it. He was collecting various articles of our dirty clothing and adding it to his "nest." There's nothing like some nice, smelly, unwashed laundry to help a guy relax at the end of a busy day. No wonder Spencer was so content with his new home!

Hopefully, the Evacuation Game in the previous chapter prompted you to think about all the things you own. Often, we keep a lot more than we actually need or even like. Why do we do this?

Is it possible we collect for the same reasons Spencer stole dirty laundry for his bed—to hold on to our loved ones through the long night in the kennel? To surround ourselves with the "essence" of those we love?

We do hold on, don't we? We hold on to our kid's child-hoods, to happy periods in the past, to our youth, to loved ones who have gone before us. We also hold onto things because of guilt, because we think we might use or repair them someday, and because we forget we have them. But a lot of our holding on has to do with memories. Photographs are one way of remembering, but there's nothing like actually holding the wedding gown, the military medals, those dried flowers from the prom or the baby's baptismal outfit, is there?

There is comfort in the stuff we collect. It can feel like a fluffy old quilt to wrap ourselves in when the world gets to be too much.

But the things we keep have a downside: They turn on us. Things start falling out of closets on our heads. We can't find the key or the wallet or the checkbook. We become allergic to the dust, and we can't keep the house clean. New items don't fit into any drawer or closet.

Clutter steals away our time and saps our energy. It takes time and energy to keep it, to take care of it, to find things we need buried under it. Clutter costs us money when we buy something we already have because we forgot we had it. Clutter makes it hard to relax. It screams for attention, like a cranky child who has been dragged around on errands all day. "Do something about this," your house screams. Maybe your spouse or children scream the same thing. (Of course, *they* don't have any clutter. Everything *they* have is needed and useful!)

Clutter does another insidious thing. In a society in which the "ideal" house would qualify as a mansion a few decades ago, we build or move to bigger houses because society expects this as we become more successful. Perhaps the real reason we "move up" is because clutter makes our houses smaller. How many of us believe we have outgrown our current house when the truth is that we need to clean out some clutter?

Clutter doesn't just take up room. Whole areas of our houses "disappear" because we can't look at them anymore. Soon, those areas become like black holes in space. I have a huge covered

· · • · ·
33

patio (thirty by twelve feet) with a lovely Mexican tile floor. During remodeling, it was getting smaller and smaller as my contractor used it to store lumber and supplies. When he was finished, it was my duty to sort through the leftovers, keep what could be used and throw the rest away. I put it off for months. What a joy it was to clear it out and rediscover over three hundred square feet of living space.

We all know people with whole rooms closed off and used as storerooms for all their extra junk. That is a lot of unavailable space, square footage we discount when we think about our houses. Most of us don't need more storage. We need less to store.

Here is a good rule about clutter: It is valid to keep things important to us, but remember the cost. Everything we keep has to be maintained, takes up space and uses time and energy. If we love it and really want it, if we would take it along to another planet if that angel knocked on the door, then it is reasonable to keep it. Use the results of the Evacuation Game to make decisions about what to keep or eliminate. Whatever did not make your list is fair game for the giveaway pile, the garbage bin or the recycling center.

Start by forming a mental picture of how you would like your home to look. See each room as clean, beautiful and functional with the family's favorite things displayed where they are enjoyed. Think about how you would like to use each room. Do you envision sitting in your sunny living room listening to music and reading the Sunday paper? Sipping coffee in the kitchen? Being able to pursue a hobby in its own special area? Gathering with friends and family in the backyard?

Envision every closet and cabinet and drawer in the house. "I'd like to see all my clothes when I open this closet." "I'd like to find a pen that works when I open this drawer." "I want to keep my preserved butterfly collection in this drawer."

See yourself functioning easily in every area of your house, unstressed, relaxed and able to find anything. Don't worry about how this is going to happen. Just *think* about it now. All accomplishments start with a vision. The plan and action happen later.

We will discuss the details of clearing out in the next two chapters. For now, make a commitment to clear out anything not helping in life, anything old and no longer useful, anything not loved—in other words, clutter.

QUESTIONS FOR REFLECTION

1. Do you think you keep things for the same reason Spencer made his nest, to comfort you with familiar things and the memories of loved ones and good times?

2. What is the downside of having too many things? Have you experienced some of the problems listed in this chapter (losing things, no room in closets)? Is your house becoming smaller and smaller because of clutter?

3. Would you clear out your clutter if you knew how?

ACTIVITY

Write out what you have envisioned for your surroundings. Next, write out your commitment. What general goal do you want to achieve? Pick a date to start "clearing out clutter." Then pick the first room to start decluttering.

NOTE
[1] Andrew M. Greeley, *When Life Hurts: Healing Themes From the Gospels* (Chicago: Thomas More, 1988), pp. 114–115.

CHAPTER SIX

CLEARING OUT THE CLUTTER:
THE GRIEF AND THE GLORY

God is a God not of disorder but of peace.
—1 Corinthians 14:33

It's time to get practical about this clutter problem we all share. First, though, what is the connection to our spirituality? Does God really care if our houses are cluttered? Actually, yes. If it bothers us, it bothers God. We can be so connected to our physical possessions that it causes great grief to give them up (thus the title to this chapter). Clutter interferes with our relationships, especially our relationship with God.

Clearing out the clutter, as mundane as it may seem, is really a sacred task. There is a connection between the messes we make and our spirituality. But first we must decide we really have too many things, possessions that do not help us be the people we want to be.

I learned to get organized by watching certain television shows. They helped me move from a eighteen-hundred-square-foot home with a full basement crammed with eighteen years' worth of junk, to my current twelve-hundred-square-foot home with no basement. This took over a year. How did this miracle come about?

- Six pickups by and drop-offs at various charities
- Five weeks sitting at a shredder destroying thirty years' worth of canceled checks and bank statements
- Four garage sales
- Three county recycling events where I dropped off appliances, a computer, three (yes, three) broken console TVs and boxes full of toxic chemicals
- Two pickup-truckloads of furniture carted away by my college-age kids
- And finally (drum roll, please!) one trip to a university thirty-five miles away to drop off thirty years' worth of *National Geographic* magazines

I should have been ready to move then, right? Wrong. I used more than my allotted space in the moving van and ended up giving away several more carloads to charities and friends. The last two garbage pickups before my move netted piles at the curb about twenty feet long, and I left my neighbors with a similar batch to put out after I left. I left a bottle of expensive wine and a nice note for them. I hope they have forgiven me.

After arriving in Arizona, my brother came to help. The trailer with my things arrived, he opened the door and he mentioned something to the effect that I may have brought a tiny bit more than one person could possibly need in a lifetime.

I was too tired to slap him.

If you are at the beginning of a huge job like mine, there is hope. I did it—mostly alone—and I survived. It does take time. It also helps to move or pretend you are moving.

Here are the steps I used, or steps I would have used if I had thought of them. Hindsight is so wonderful.

CLEARING OUT THE CLUTTER

1. Extract the essentials.

Extract the things you must not lose, and place them in a safe area we'll call your "Launching Pad." This would include things on your Evacuation Game list, important papers like your passport, and the dog. Other items to place on your Launching Pad are keys, bills to be paid, calendar items, mail to go out, library books and anything else urgent.

2. Remove everything.

Once you extract your essentials, remove everything from the area you are clearing and sort it into piles, boxes or bags. Basic categories include "Keep," "Give Away," "Throw Away," "Recycle" and "?" for those things you feel ambivalent about. This last pile should be placed with the giveaway pile. There is a good reason we feel ambivalent about keeping certain items. We really want to be rid of them! This "?" pile will mostly be gone by the time you are done.

Professional organizers on TV often clear whole rooms of everything, furniture, wall hangings and all. This is because they plan elaborate changes, including fancy storage units, new furniture and wild paint colors. Feel free to do this, or just clean the room well. You may want to rearrange the furniture and rethink the wall hangings, but that is optional.

3. Put things back.

Once you have sorted through everything, the next step is to put back *only* the things you have decided to keep (in other words, only one of the four piles). When all is said and done you should theoretically have one-fourth of the room to replace. Another helpful task is to put things back in the order of their importance; you may find that you are able to reduce the contents of the room even further by giving away or throwing out the things that you regarded as least important. It might surprise you!

4. Rethink everything.
When the room or closet or drawer looks right and feels comfortable, when drawers, closets and cabinets are about half-full: STOP. Rethink everything else you used to keep there. Maybe you don't need the extra furniture, pictures and knickknacks. If you were clearing out your kitchen cabinets, evaluate how many food storage containers, drinking cups, baking pans and serving pieces one person or family really needs.

5. Remove the clutter permanently.
Now comes the fun part. Deliver your donations to a thrift store or charity, visit your local recycling center and put the garbage out. I have a friend who periodically puts all his give-aways on his front lawn with a big sign: "FREE." He lives on a well-traveled road near a high school. His lawn is generally empty by sundown.

You may also have a garage sale, but only if all of the following apply: (1) You think garage sales are fun and do not care how little money you make. (2) You have a minimum of one week to devote to it. (3) You live on a reasonably busy street or have a willing friend who does. (4) You arrange for any leftovers to be picked up by or delivered to a charity immediately after the sale. No bringing things back into the house.

6. Get help from a friend.
We all have messy friends who need this kind of help as much as we do. Take turns working on each other's houses. The great thing about having friends help is that they give us an objective view of what we are holding on to. Remind each other how much each of you will love your houses when it's all over. A

friend will keep us going so we actually get the job done and don't give up halfway through.

CLEARING OUT THE "OTHER" STUFF

Although the aforementioned steps will help you declutter, I do realize that it is easier said than done and that there are some things that are just difficult to part with for sentimental reasons. And there are also things we hold onto, because, frankly, they are a pain to get rid of—electronics, old appliances and chemicals, to name a few. These are probably the most challenging situations you will deal with when decluttering, but the following are some simple suggestions to help you through the crunch.

How to Part With Keepsakes, Collections and Memorabilia

The most challenging clutter problem is when it comes time to part with grown children's keepsakes, collections and memorabilia.

When I moved to Arizona, my sons were all living in college apartments and moved frequently. Because I am a good mom and my boys are not yet settled in life, I agreed to move their treasures with me. Their "loot" includes a baseball card collection, large pieces of art, trophies, favorite books and shoe boxes of boy-type treasures I am not allowed to ask about. This is okay with me right now, but will not be ten years from now. There comes a time to say to our children, "Come and get this stuff, or it's going in the trash." To keep children's things for them temporarily is fine, but don't keep their things after they are married or over thirty years old. Pick a cutoff date. If your children will not come and get their treasures, they must not want them. Get rid of the clutter with a clear conscience.

Collections and memorabilia are difficult categories. My feeling about collections is the larger the collection, the less sense it makes. Most of us start a collection by falling in love with a particular piece. Then we think we would like more of them. People find out we have a collection, so they start buying us pieces. The collection gets too big or we lose interest, but we can't just throw it out. We paid a lot for this clutter.

My advice? (You bought this book, so I know it's not unsolicited!) Don't even start a collection. If it is too late, find a way to pare it down. Keep that first piece you fell in love with, photograph the rest, and turn the whole lot over to an auction house or someone who sells things for others on eBay. A charity thrift store might be thrilled to get your collection, and you get a tax deduction.

Memories are another tricky category. The best way to keep sentimental items under control is to keep *one* item from a category: One baby outfit per child, one present from a special anniversary, one doll from childhood, one antique from the parents' or grandparents' house.

. . . . .

41

How to Get Rid of Things Responsibly

When decluttering there is a temptation to throw everything in the trash. If it is old, broken and past its usefulness, go ahead. But if it is still in good shape—"gently used" as the classifieds often list goods—offer it to a needy family or friend that you know could use it. Take the time to bring it to a charity or call them for pickup.

Appliances, computers and electronics should be recycled. Our garbage dumps are filled with things made of metals and plastics, which could be used again. Up to 95 percent of appliances are made of recyclable materials. Call your county recycling agency for places that recycle. If it can't help you, search the Internet for local establishments that are willing to take your goods. One website I recommend is www.GreenerChoices.org.

If you have toxic items like garden and household chemicals, turn them over to your county for proper disposal. Many counties have household chemical recycling days. The ones in which I participated were educational. Everyone was dressed in protective gear from head to foot. They put my seemingly innocent waste into huge metal barrels with alarming symbols on the side. I think twice now before I buy chemicals and bring them into my house.

Keeping our houses, closets, drawers and cabinets clutter-free is an ongoing commitment. Once an area has been pared down and looks the way we envisioned, it becomes much easier to keep it that way. We must resist the urge to add anything. We must promise ourselves we will get rid of something before buying any new item.

THE GRIEF

There is grief in getting rid of things. We hold onto them for a reason. They remind us of past phases of life, of our youth, of our kids' childhoods. Even when we want to clear out, even when we are ecstatic over our newfound space and freedom, there is a bittersweet feeling.

After my last garage sale before I moved to Arizona, I went down to the basement, which was finally cleared out. As I stood there congratulating myself on a job well done, a feeling of sadness flooded me. The exercise equipment all of us had used, the drum set the boys had banged on incessantly, even those old televisions we had watched together, reminded me of a life I no longer had. The kids were grown, and I was about to sell the house and move on. Yes, there is grief.

THE GLORY

But there is also glory. My grief lasted a few minutes. My happiness in the present is continual. I love my new life and am happy to have so much less to take care of. I can find things now, and I have much less to clean. This leaves me free to do other things like writing, relaxing and playing.

Our possessions should make us soar. They should enhance our lives, make us happy, inspire our love and creativity.

Our belongings should not bog us down and make slaves of us. We should be surrounded with beauty, with things reminding us we are God's children.

Anything else should be removed.

So go ahead and clear out. Feel any grief you have to feel, but then enjoy!

ACTIVITY

Fill out the following section that will help you identify your goals for decluttering your environment. Check any answers that apply:

_____ To walk into any room in my house or open any closet or drawer and know what is there and why.

_____ To know where to find anything in my house in a reasonable period of time, without having other things fall on me while I am looking for it.

_____ To have only the things which I need, use or love.

_____ To be free of clutter and to be able to feel that freedom.

_____ To free up the time I now spend taking care of my possessions.

_____ To be at peace, because God really is a God of order and peace.

CHAPTER SEVEN

The Paper Monster—Stuff

> Here's how I define "stuff": anything you have allowed into
> your psychological or physical world that doesn't belong
> where it is, but for which you haven't yet determined a
> desired outcome and the next action step.
> —David Allen, *Getting Things Done: The Art of Stress-Free
> Productivity*[1]

What is "stuff"? We use the word loosely; it can mean almost anything.

I like David Allen's definition. Stuff is obligations, duties, commitments, responsibilities. Stuff may be a large project, a simple phone call (if there is such a thing), a letter we haven't written, an unbalanced checkbook. Most stuff is represented by pieces of paper. If we have such trouble organizing our knickknacks, cabinets and sock drawers, the papers lying around our houses—our stuff—threatens to send us into spasms of despair or rage. It seems hopeless.

I once took a whole year to straighten out my son's dentist bill. I wrote it on numerous to-do lists and postponed doing it. When I finally made the phone call and spoke to a nice lady in India, we got the problem solved in a few minutes. I am very organized these days. I throw out my junk and keep my house neat, but little chores like that phone call can undo me.

Paperwork is a difficult problem for anyone who wants a neat, uncluttered life. Sometimes we actually get it under control. Then the mail comes and the fragile balance is upset. We can't simply throw it all out. Credit card offers have to be shredded or someone may dive into our dumpsters, sign our names and steal our identity. We might need that pizza coupon. Bank statements must be reconciled and filed. We have to read this. We have to make a decision about it. We need to make a phone call to straighten out a problem. We are overdue for our dentist appointment, and the dog is overdue for shots.

The most frustrating part of trying to have an orderly house is that there are people and computers out there that have our names, know about our good (or bad) credit ratings and are determined to be our "friends." Each piece of paper they send represents an action we have to take, even if that action is to toss it. The pieces of paper we decide to keep make life very complicated.

What do we do about this?

Since I am an avid paper collector (writers need to keep things, I say), and have found a way to control it, I know there is a viable solution to the problem. And it does not involve moving to a mountaintop with no forwarding address.

We all have multiple facets of life we must manage. Writers like me tend to keep extensive files of things we might need to use someday. I had no organized way to keep all this "stuff," so it was in boxes and bags all over my house. But after I read Allen's book, *Getting Things Done: The Art of Stress-Free Productivity,* I was able to implement a productive paper-filing system. This was a two-month-long project, but from the first day I had new hope. It could be done. After making all those files, I learned to manage my "actionable" papers, the things we all have lying around representing phone calls to make, things to do on the Internet, letters to write, finances to manage, projects we would like to do. This has been a slower process. We will discuss this phase of paper control, which is actually work control, in chapter ten.

HOW TO IMPLEMENT A FILING SYSTEM

★ *For a complete description of how to implement a filing-system, read* Getting Things Done: The Art of Stress-Free Productivity *by David Allen.*

Supplies
- Three boxes of letter-sized manila file folders (not hanging folders)
- A label maker
- Several refill spools of 1/2" white labels
- Garbage bags
- File boxes
- 3" x 3" Sticky notes
- Tape
- Stapler
- Pens
- Markers
- Scissors

You will need the following items later:
- Three-ring binder
- Looseleaf paper
- Section dividers

(Eventually, you will need filing cabinets for the new files, but don't buy them until you know how much drawer space you need. When you do buy filing cabinets, buy sturdy ones.)

Begin to File

1. Find all your stray papers or as much as will fit in a large laundry basket.

2. Fill the basket by sweeping everything into it from piles, boxes and bags on your desktops and counters, in your closets and under your beds. One full laundry basket is more than enough for one evening's worth of filing.

3. Either set up a comfortable workstation at a table or desk, or do what I did and plop down in front of the TV on the floor. This is very important: Turn on pleasant music or find something inane on the television (how hard will that be?). I spent many happy hours making files while watching old movies and reruns of my favorite sitcoms. The hours flew by as the files piled up, the recycling bag filled and my laundry basket emptied. I really enjoyed this. If this does not sound like fun, wait. I have helped friends start this system. They got enthusiastic about making files as soon as they saw their chaos replaced by order.

4. Pick up the first piece of paper on top of the pile. Look at it and ask: What is this? Defining each piece of paper helps clarify why you kept it and what you need to do with it. If the paper represents something "actionable," make a file for it as I explain in step 6. If it does not require any action, make a decision to keep it or throw it away. You may keep anything you like for any reason.

5. Make files for each item you want to keep using your label maker. It's okay to have one piece of paper in a file folder. Name your files whatever you will remember later. I have a file for humorous stories and Internet jokes. I call it "Jokes." Nothing is too silly to warrant a file. Also, file things in categories: "Insurance—Health," "Insurance—Car," "Insurance— Homeowners" rather than "Homeowners Insurance," etc.

Your files will start to accumulate. Your paper clutter piles will disappear. You will feel wonderful.

6. When you come across an "actionable" article, put it into its own file folder and keep it on the Launching Pad you established while reading the last chapter. Make files for phone calls, Internet, errands and things to write on your calendar or in your address book. You may also have an "Agghhhhh!!" file for those things lost in your paper piles, like last month's water bill.

7. Make a commitment to continue this process until it is done, until every scrap of paper in your home has gone through this scrutiny and ended up in your new files, on your Launching Pad or in your trash.

It took weeks of going through my house, finding yet another pile, box or bag of paper "goodies," putting it in the laundry basket, and turning it into files. I found things I had lost years before. I cleared whole shelves in my closets and most of the surfaces in my house. Now I am able to find things because every piece of paper in my house has its own file.

GOD EVEN CARES ABOUT PAPER

Paper clutter is one of the most frustrating forms of clutter. It represents duties, unfinished business, delayed dreams and guilt. It takes up room in our minds and on all the surfaces in our homes.

God cares about our paper clutter because God cares about us. God knows what all those pieces of paper are doing to our mental health. What affects our minds affects our spirits. God wants us to be as free as possible to love one another and to be creative, to fulfill our destinies as God's children. Paper clutter often interferes.

It is amazing what power a piece of paper can have. But

"stuff" is a reality in our world. God wants us to learn how to deal with it, because God wants us to have peace and order in our lives.

ACTIVITY

Fill out the following section that will help you discern your plan for managing the paper "stuff" that comes into your life. Check any answers that apply:

_____ To have a simple system for managing paper that works and that I trust.

_____ To be able to put my hand on any piece of paper I need, when I need it, whether it is as mundane as an Internet joke or as important as my 2002 tax return for an audit.

_____ To never again have piles of paper all over my house.

_____ To never again be late paying a bill or filing a tax return because I misplaced a piece of paper.

_____ To have only the paper that I need, use or love.

_____ To be free of paper clutter and to be able to feel that freedom.

_____ To free up the time I now spend taking care of my paper mess to _____

_____

_____.

_____ To be at peace, because God really is a God of order and peace.

NOTE

[1] David Allen, *Getting Things Done: The Art of Stress-Free Productivity* (New York: Penguin, 2001), p. 17.

SECTION THREE

PRODUCTIVITY WITHOUT CLUTTER

We spend a great deal of our waking hours working. In fact, many of us spend *every* waking hour doing some kind of work. In our culture work and productivity are elevated almost to the status of gods.

Work is necessary to us as human beings. But how well do we work? And how do we know when we are overworking, slipping into workaholism? These are the themes of this section.

First, we consider the list. I love making lists; many of you do, too. Are lists good for us or defeating? We discuss workaholism, both the traditional "Type A" workaholic and what I call the "lazy workaholic." We will also discuss some methods for managing our lists. Finally, we consider the question: Does God help those who help themselves? How much of our work is completely our responsibility? How much should we rely on God?

CHAPTER EIGHT

I LOVE A LIST

Life is not about checking off items on lists....
Not everyone needs a to-do list.
Some of us need "don't do" lists.
—T. Alexander Anderson, *The Gift of Time*[1]

In spite of Anderson's statement above (which I would have thought of as blasphemy a few years ago), I love to make lists.

There's nothing like settling down on a long winter evening with lots of paper and pens and writing or rewriting all my to-do lists. I have been known to actually keep lists of the things I completed on old lists.

A great to-do list includes everything I might possibly want to do—ever. This would include chores, house projects (short-term and far into the future), hobbies, exercise, diets, "how I want the kids to turn out," trips I would love to take, even learning Spanish and Russian (not simultaneously). And, yes, work-related things and mundane things like paying bills and balancing the checkbook.

CREATING THE MOTHER OF ALL LISTS

On a blank sheet of paper make the most comprehensive to-do list ever. Make categories so you don't forget anything: family, house, career, hobbies, school, financial, pets, letters to write, medical, dental, "someday I'd like to…" and most importantly, a category for God. Look over your list and think about how you feel the more you look at it. Is the list starting to turn on you, accuse you? The elation doesn't last long, does it?

David Allen says we feel like this because our brains think all these things should be done *right now*. Anytime we have more than one thing to do it causes feelings of failure because we cannot do more than one thing at a time. Allen spends a lot of time in his consulting business teaching people to get things out of their brains and onto paper or into some other external system. Even so, he admits that the traditional to-do list does not work as a way to get things done.

My usual reaction after making a list is an overwhelmed sigh and the urge to take a nap. Lists may tell us *what*, but they don't tell us *how*—how to find the time and energy to do everything, how to prioritize, how to get started.

Why do we make lists? We hope our lists will help us remember things, but we often forget where our lists are! We list because life is confusing and complicated. Creating a list makes us feel we are taking control again. We may list because we hope to be done someday. Then we will begin the lives we would be living if we didn't have all this stuff to do.

There may be a deeper reason for listmaking. If we have a long to-do list going, it means we are not useless. We matter. We have things to do. We are important to the world—see that list? We will never run out of work and become bored. Having nothing to do is a horrifying thought in our culture. Our society equates doing with worthiness. Only people who are old, sick or otherwise useless have nothing to do. Our lists prove we are not one of them.

There are negatives to the list habit, but there is also a good side. Lists can be a way of dreaming on paper, which is a good thing to do. Some claim that writing down dreams as lists or journal entries is beneficial. We accomplish a lot without thinking about it, if we articulate our goals on paper. Author Henriette Anne Klauser has devoted a whole book to this idea called *Write It Down, Make It Happen*. She tells stories of people who were brave enough to express their dreams in great detail on paper and watched these things start to happen all around them.

I have experienced this phenomenon myself. Have you? My dream of moving to Arizona and writing full-time began as a dream on paper. We do remember things if we have written them down, especially if our lists include our dreams and hopes for the future.

So, lists can be good or bad. What is a list-maker to do?

After years of making lists and getting frustrated by them, I have found a better way to make my lists. It satisfies my list-making inclination, and it almost eliminates the guilt I previously felt about my huge to-do lists.

The best way to deal with the listmaking urge is to go ahead and make a big one. Include *everything* you dream of doing, not just the things you must do. Your lists should be kept in a safe place. Remember that loose-leaf notebook you bought when buying your filing supplies (see page 46)? That is where you keep your lists. Divide it into general categories: Work, house projects, budget and miscellaneous items. Any project involving more than one step *gets its own page* listing the steps to accomplish it. Include telephone numbers and other vital information. This is your new Action Notebook, your new to-do list. It should be reviewed regularly, preferably weekly. It will be used for looking up information, remembering the steps involved in projects and honoring your dreams. It satisfies the listmaking urge in a positive way.

But the Action Notebook is *not* what we use to determine daily tasks. Our *daily* to-do lists should fit on a 3" x 3" sticky note. Personally, I cannot handle more than three items per day. That is just about right for a my daily to-do list. If your daily tasks do not fit on a sticky note, you are probably trying to do too much. (Tiny writing does not count!)

We often try to do too much in one day. This sets us up for failure. Think about it: If there are ten items on a list and only four get done, we have only accomplished 40 percent of our goals. If we list three and do four, we have done 125 percent. Planning to do no more than three things a day ensures feelings of success. We only plan what we know is possible today.

So if you have the list habit, go ahead and make all the lists you want. Include everything you must do or want to do. Break down each item into all the steps involved. Keep these lists in their own special Action Notebook. When planning your daily work, look over your Action Notebook and make short, achievable lists of no more than three items. And just for fun, take T. Alexander Anderson's advice. Make a list of things you *don't* want to do. Then don't do them!

ACTIVITIES

1. If you made a list while reading this chapter, look it over now and think about what is wrong with it. Does it include enough detail about *how* to accomplish each task? Does it include your dreams and other positive things you would love to do? Or does it include only heavy obligations you dread?

2. If you have not done so, buy a loose-leaf binder and a pad of sticky notes. Begin to make two kinds of lists from now on: An "everything" list in your new Action Notebook and a daily to-do list of three items on a sticky note.

NOTE
[1] Anderson, p. 77.

CHAPTER NINE

WORKAHOLISM: TYPE A AND THE LAZY WORKAHOLIC

Consider how you have fared. You have sown much,
and harvested little; you eat, but you never have enough;
you drink, but you never have your fill; you clothe
yourselves, but no one is warm; and you that earn wages
earn wages to put them into a bag with holes.

—Haggai 1:5–6

The prophet Haggai wrote these words over five hundred years
before Jesus was born. The Israelites had recently returned from
exile in Babylon. The temple in Jerusalem was in ruins, but they
put off rebuilding it. They were busy resettling in a homeland
many were too young to remember. There were droughts and
crop failures. The temple was not a priority; they were trying to
make their lives better, trying to get ahead.

Does this sound familiar? Our circumstances are different,
but we feel the pinch of our economy, don't we? Gas and food

prices keep going up. It is difficult to find a reasonably priced house or apartment. Many of us do not feel secure about our employment. Who can blame us if we work long hours, if work becomes the center of our existence?

Most of us are workaholics. This is not a scientific statement, just an observation. Our culture expects us to be workaholics. It calls this productivity and worships it in every area of life: in the workplace, at home, at our children's schools, even at church. Everyone should be busy and doing many things. The company will succeed if we work hard enough. We must have beautiful homes everyone will envy. Our children must be accepted into the right colleges in order to be worthy in society (and so that we as parents are deemed good ones for making it possible). The parish will succeed and many people will join and be saved—if we work hard enough.

If most of us are workaholics, let's define workaholism. I believe there are two types: The Type A workaholic we are all familiar with, and what I call the "lazy (Type B) workaholic," who is not lazy at all.

The Type A workaholic—much maligned in modern psychology, but admired in the corporate world and in the culture—throws herself into work to the exclusion of everything else. There is never enough to do. She is addicted to activity. She is uncomfortable sitting still. She never gets tired and hates to stop even to sleep.

We all know Type A workaholics; we may be one or married to one. We have heard about the dangers of this type of workaholism: heart attack, stroke, divorce, estrangement from children.

I believe there is a second type of workaholic. No one talks about this, but I believe most of us qualify. This is the "lazy" workaholic—the Type B workaholic.

I am a Type B workaholic. I was labeled as "lazy" by teachers and "slow moving" by family members. No one knew how much effort I was putting into trying to be a Type A workaholic!

A lazy, Type B workaholic is a "wanna-be" workaholic, a workaholic-in-waiting. We share the same set of values and the belief that "We must produce," but we don't have the energy to be true Type A workaholics. Maybe we were labeled "lazy" as youngsters because we didn't produce enough good grades, science projects or spectacular touchdowns. Our society expects all of us to do what Type A workaholics do. We admire the Type A; anyone else does not measure up.

We "lazy" workaholics back into tasks reluctantly. We feel we must be more productive, but our hearts aren't in it. We make lots of unfinished to-do lists. If we are not addicted to activity, we are trying to please someone who is. We are exhausted a lot, mostly from worry. We consider ourselves poor performers, and teachers, parents and Type A workaholics agree. We place heavy burdens on ourselves. If one day goes well, we think all future days must be the same; that should become the norm. If we do well one day, we raise the stakes. "If I can do that, why can't I do this, this and this?"

I have relinquished my membership and medals in the Workaholics Club. Oh, I still miss the adrenaline rush of making impossible lists and rushing around to see how much I get done. Sometimes I feel guilty when I put two or three things on my daily list, get them done early and relax the rest of the day. Sometimes.

Strangely, I am more productive now. I get more done in less time, with a lot less angst than when I rushed, worried, pushed and beat myself up.

True productivity is a function of feeling good about ourselves, staying in touch with God and practicing moderation in all things, even how much we expect to produce in a day.

Real productivity is invisible. If we were to watch Einstein when he was thinking about the Theory of Relativity, or a writer getting ready to write, or an artist getting ready to paint, we would not see much. In fact, we might think they were half-asleep. Our culture does not respect people who sit around looking like they are taking a nap, especially during office hours. The usual reaction of coworkers and family members is to walk up to a person in this state, talk to them and make sure they are alive and awake.

Here is a good analogy. When we type instructions on a computer and press "enter," the computer does not run around cleaning the house or office! It sits quietly and does what it was told to do. A friend of mine says programmers have made computers blink and whir because their silence while working would be unnerving. We would kick them and scream at them because we would believe they were broken. To us, activity equals productivity; no activity means something is wrong. Is it any wonder our culture does not value intellectual or creative people? They don't seem to be doing enough.

If we need permission to stop being "productive" and to do the deep but unproductive-looking work of the mind or heart, remember Einstein and our computers. And if we need a higher authority's permission, here it is: "Be still, and know that I am God!" (Psalm 46:10).

Being still so that we can pray, think, plan and even brood is the most important facet of productivity. How many times do we tell ourselves there is no time to pray or to stop and think before we begin work? We have deadlines. We are overwhelmed. We'd better get to work right now. We will eat later, pray later, pay attention to loved ones later. This is another cultural lie. It is the mantra of the workaholic, Type A or Type B. The truth is this: We cannot put off prayer, relationships and taking care of our bodies because we have too much to do.

The greatest thing each of us offers the world is *ourselves*, not a whirlwind of activity. People all around us are starving for love. We live with some of them; others live right in our neighborhoods. People need our company, our presence and our comfort.

Let us stop sowing but not harvesting; eating but never having enough; drinking but staying thirsty; worrying about our clothes but never being warm. Let's especially stop putting everything we earn into bags with holes.

QUESTIONS FOR REFLECTION

1. Are you a workaholic? If so, are you a Type A or Type B? Did this surprise you?

2. What are some of your "issues" about why you work so much? Is it the economy? Your job? Providing for your family? Do you just feel more comfortable doing something rather than sitting still?

3. Who needs you right now? Are you neglecting this person because of work?

ACTIVITY

List all the people who are important in your life. Are you spending enough time with them or is work getting in the way? List their names here and ask God how you might reach out to them more often.

_____

_____

_____

CHAPTER TEN

A Better Way to Be Productive

Productive people have a love affair with time.... They get
more from time than others, seem to know how to use time
much better than nonproductive people—so much so that
they can waste immense quantities of time and still be
enormously creative and productive.

—Kenneth Atchity, *A Writer's Time: A Guide to the Creative
Process from Vision through Revision*[1]

A Love Affair With Time

What a concept.

The first time I read this quote, it seemed impossible, something an alien from another planet might recommend. But
Atchity's words filled me with a deep longing. I could not get
the idea out of my head. Was it possible?

Back then work terrified me. A chronic Type B workaholic,
I experienced a lot of failure and felt inadequate to do whatever
the world was expecting. I was married to a Type A workaholic
who seemed to get a lot done. I was surrounded by people at

work and in the neighborhood who seemed to know how to get a lot done. Everyone else seemed to know something I didn't about working, having a beautiful home, living an efficient life. What was wrong with me? I should have been doing better!

I had been writing for ten years. This was a love-hate relationship. I wrote well when I got down to it but procrastinated until deadlines loomed. I was afraid of the inevitable writer's blocks, but I never just stopped and thought it out. I met my deadlines at the cost of pain and exhaustion. Housework, projects and volunteer work produced the same type of dread.

Working this way is not exclusive to writers and other artistic types. People from all walks of life really, deep down, hate to work. The people who long for retirement or wish they could make it big far outnumber those who love what they are doing and would still do it if they won the lottery.

"Work" has come to have an unpleasant association in our western minds. It denotes obligation, perhaps even a form of slavery. Corporate downsizing and a shaky economy have made things worse. Many of us are working well past our planned retirement age. Mothers who would prefer to stay at home with young children find that it is a luxury they cannot afford. People in corporate settings are doing the jobs of two or three others who were "downsized," and they feel grateful to have a job.

God never intended work to be so hateful. Even employment, our work to earn our bread and contribute to the good of society, should not be loathsome. To make matters worse, we equate almost everything we do today as work. Keeping up a home, ferrying kids to activities, having pets, volunteering at church are all work. Prayer and getting together with friends are work. Even our vacations are work. All our pleasures have become something to check off on our to-do lists, something that takes time and stresses us out.

How do we move from feeling "work equals slavery" to "a love affair with time"? It is possible if we adjust our attitude about the meaning of work. We do so by remembering the difference between "being" and "doing." We were not put here on earth to do things, to scramble around like gerbils on wheels, exhausting ourselves, getting nowhere. We were created because God had a dream in mind for each of us to become *somebody*. Our doings—our work—should flow out of that *somebody*.

FOUR SIMPLE STEPS TO BECOMING MORE PRODUCTIVE
1. We must learn to STOP.

Most of us run around faster and faster when things get hectic. We rush from task to task with no reflection. But the correct thing to do when we are pressed, hurried and harried is to *stop*. This will drive the other workaholics around us nuts, which may be good for them and entertaining for us. It will also give us time to take a few deep breaths, decide not to say what we were going to and think clearly about what we should do next.

2. We must learn to PLAN.

Stopping helps us to plan and to pray as we plan. We should plan today's activities, next week's big project, next month's vacation. Planning shortens the time our tasks take. Planning means going ahead mentally, seeing the steps we will take to reach a goal. Planning makes work less terrifying. Planning means we have already done the job in our heads before doing it with our hands. We will have a better idea how much time it will take, what we need, how much we can reasonably get accomplished today.

Planning involves "next actions." This is a David Allen (*Getting Things Done*) term. Before starting any task, we ask ourselves what the "next action" is. Let's say I have to make a phone call. Do I need to write down what I am going to say?

Do I need to find some information? Do I need to find a phone number? Do I need to find the phone book or the phone? By the time we do "next actions," the task is often half-done. This type of planning builds momentum and helps us get over the difficulty of starting a new task. Most items on our lists only include the end result. They never list all the little steps—the "next actions"—to that result. No wonder the typical to-do list does not help us.

I never did much planning during my "hate work" years. I made long lists that could never be accomplished by one human and called this planning. Listing and planning are totally different. When I began to take time to plan, however long it took at first, I began to accomplish things. Work became possible, even enjoyable.

3. We must learn to PRIORITIZE.

Do this by simply looking over your current projects and appointments. The important things stand out. Choose three of them to put on your daily to-do note. If you have several deadlines or complicated projects at one time, write the individual steps for each task on separate index cards. Shuffle these around and choose a few to do each day, based on their importance and your energy level. Obviously, do the most vital things first. Eventually, some cards will be eliminated because time runs out. Most projects get done when we run out of time to fuss with them.

Prioritizing means making choices. We cannot do anything else while doing today's tasks. Therefore, it is silly to think about what we are not doing or to rush through one job to get to another. Hurrying through our work to get to our other work means we will never enjoy our work. We will also never do anything well.

4. Finally, we must learn to TRUST.

We trust that we can make good choices about our work. We trust that today's work is really enough, that our other obligations can wait. We trust that God does not expect more of us than is humanly possible, even if the rest of the world does.

Let us remember God never gives us more than we are able to handle. If we are constantly overwhelmed, God is not the culprit. Either we are taking on too much, or others are expecting too much of us. If they are, it is up to us to protect ourselves and educate them. It is also up to us to say "no" when appropriate. No one can take advantage of us unless we allow them to.

WORK=BEING STILL

Work is not merely activity; work can also mean being still. It is being quiet with God, planning, dreaming, imagining, creating. Work should bring about its own satisfaction. It should lead to pleasant absorption and immersion. People who know how to work say that time stands still, even disappears, while they are working. It does not matter if we are washing dishes, painting a still life, writing a corporate report, doing physical labor or writing a book. Work should be its own pleasure.

Yes, work used to terrify me, and I often hated it. I have different goals now than I did then. I want to be the person Kenneth Atchity describes in this chapter's opening. I want to work, be enormously productive and waste incredible amounts of time while I'm doing it!

QUESTIONS FOR REFLECTION

1. What does it mean to be productive? Does your work seem like a sentence to slavery, or is it pleasurable? Would you quit if you suddenly had enough money?

2. How do you plan your work? Do the suggestions in this chapter make sense to you? If so, can you start implementing them?

ACTIVITIES

1. Use the first ten or fifteen minutes of your workday to look ahead. What three things do you want to accomplish? How will you do them? Imagine yourself going through each task.
2. Do this David Allen "next action" exercise. Think of one item on your to-do list particularly worrisome to you right now. Write it down and think of all the "next actions" associated with it. Look over your list. Does it seem more doable and less frustrating now? Can you see yourself starting it?

NOTE

[1] Kenneth Atchity, *A Writer's Time: A Guide to the Creative Process from Vision through Revision* (New York: Norton, 1986), p. xiv.

CHAPTER ELEVEN

COWORKERS WITH GOD

> In a way, it would be easier to depend on God for every-
> thing or depend on God for nothing. ... But God chooses
> to treat us like equals, demanding that we do our part to the
> best of our abilities and leave the rest to him.
> —Andrew M. Greeley, *When Life Hurts*[1]

GOD HELPS THOSE...

How many of us believe the expression "God helps those who
help themselves" is actually Scripture? It is not. That little adage
is part of our cultural religion. If we believe it, perhaps we feel
we are on our own or must prove ourselves to God. Maybe God
looks to see how much effort we put forth before helping us out.
Do we really believe that God stands aside, watches us struggle
and intervenes only when we are drowning? If so, not a very nice
God, the one we believe in.

There are two places in Scripture where the apostle Peter
went out and fished all night and caught nothing (Luke 5:4–11
and John 21:1–11). Both times Jesus appeared on the shore in the

morning and told Peter where to lower his net for a huge catch of fish. Have you ever "fished all night and caught nothing"? Most of us have. It may be why the "God helps those who help themselves" saying became popular. Why does God make us go through troubles; why let us "fish all night" and wait until morning to help us out?

This is the spiritual side of the issue of work: Which part of my life's work is mine and which is God's? We perform all kinds of feats and stress ourselves out, trying to make things happen. Sometimes God takes over matters when we come to the end of ourselves and ask for help (usually the only time we ask). The fish, it turns out, were swimming right alongside the boat all along. Other times God does not appear, and the project fails or we give up on it. What is the lesson here?

Sometimes, like Peter, we will fish all night, putting in a lot of effort with little to show for it, before God answers our prayers. God may be teaching us to trust. When we finally give it up and turn it over to God, things start to happen. Sometimes, I suspect, God is trying to answer our prayers, but we are too anxious, even frenzied. For all we know, Peter rowed around frantically all night, moving to a new place when he didn't catch any fish immediately. Maybe it was only when he stopped, exhausted, in the morning that the fish were able to catch up to him.

...WHO HELP THEMSELVES

But think what it would be like if God never expected anything of us. What if God gave us everything we needed and wanted without any effort on our part? No doubt, there are times we wish that were true. Mostly, it would offend us, just like it offended us as kids when our parents did too much for us. Why? We know better. We want better for ourselves. We want to make our own mistakes; we want to do our own growing up; we want respect.

No matter how much we say God should do it all, we really want to be active participants in our own lives, in this creation and even in our salvation. We humans thrive on work and responsibility. God made us this way.

We also thrive on respect. It would not feel right if God did everything. If God did not let us problem-solve and participate in our own lives, we would never grow. God lets us "walk on our own two feet" to show us respect. There are times when we are not up to it. We take on too much; we cannot do what we wanted to. God may then step in and do the miracle, or the miracle may catch up to us. But God always applauds our efforts. There is no such thing as failure, except when we give up. God is not interested in productivity, in how much gets done. God is interested in who we are becoming. In order to "become," we must participate in the process.

So sometimes we fish all night only to fail. Then we call on God: "I can't do this. I need help." God happily fills up our boat and our whole beings with good things. Sometimes, we should ask for help a lot sooner than we do. Many times we have to do what we have to do. When we look back, we find our small, "unsuccessful" efforts had a totally different effect than we expected. Our boats have to be out on the water, and we have to have our nets ready. We have to remain calm and trust God when things are not happening as we thought they would.

Coworkers With God: A Partnership for Life

In 2004 I was desperately trying to sell my house in Ohio. I had already bought a house in Arizona, so my finances were strained to the breaking point. I tried everything: listing it with a realtor; taking it away from the realtor; trying to sell it myself; listing it with an investor who could offer buyers a land contract. I reduced the price several times. I cleaned, remodeled, carpeted, painted. Nothing happened. No one was interested in an ordinary house in a market glutted with ordinary houses. I admitted after fourteen months that I had run out of ideas and options. My second winter since listing it was approaching. The only offer I had was a bid from an investor who would turn the house into a rental. I didn't want to do that to my neighbors.

Then the miracle happened. My next-door neighbor offered me the same price as the investor's offer. He was willing to hold onto it in the hopes of selling it in the spring. This would keep the house from "going rental," protecting his and the neighbors' property values. I could now move to Arizona. I prayed God would bless him abundantly, arranged for a moving van and got out of there. My neighbor did sell the house the next summer.

We cannot rely solely upon our own skills and knowledge, nor can we give it all up and expect God to do everything. Does this mean God only helps those who help themselves? Not really. The real truth is this: *Life is meant to be a partnership between God and us in a spirit of mutual respect and trust.*

God desires a relationship in which "Be still, and know that I am God!" (Psalm 46:10) and "Work out your own salvation with fear and trembling" (Philippians 2:12) are equally true. If this sounds complicated or messy, relationships are like that. Ultimately, it is simple. If we do not know where to turn, we turn to God. If we are trying to accomplish something with no results, we ask God what to do. If it seems we are doing the right thing, but we are fishing through the night with no results, we wait for morning and put the net over the side when and where Jesus tells us to.

The one thing we should never do is believe God will only help us when we help ourselves. We are not on our own. We each have a Coworker with us every step of the way.

Questions for Reflection

1. Have you always believed God helps those who help them-selves? After reading this chapter, have you adjusted your thinking?

2. Have you ever "fished all night and caught nothing?" What were the circumstances? What did you do? What did God do?

3. Consider a time when you tried to do something completely on your own. Next, consider another time when you asked for God's help in accomplishing something. Looking back, do you view the latter as a cooperative venture with God? How did the process differ, if at all, from completing the former task?

. . • . .

Note
[1] Andrew M. Greeley. *When Life Hurts: Healing Themes from the Gospels* (Chicago: Thomas More, 1988), pp. 115–116.

SECTION FOUR

A SPIRIT WITHOUT CLUTTER

Clutter is not only a problem in our physical environment. Our minds get very cluttered with worry and resentments. Clearing out mental and spiritual clutter from our lives is the topic of Section Four.

We discuss "kicking the worry habit." There are two chapters on forgiveness, a tough topic, but very necessary for our well-being. Many of us are carrying heavy loads of mental and spiritual baggage because of past hurts we have not forgiven. Finally, we discuss the experience of waiting for God.

CHAPTER TWELVE

KICKING THE WORRY HABIT

So do not worry about tomorrow, for tomorrow will bring
worries of its own. Today's trouble is enough for today."
—Matthew 6:34

I have learned to pay attention to right now. The precise
moment I was in was always the only safe place for me.
—Julia Cameron, *The Artist's Way*[1]

THE WORRY HABIT

The first item of clutter in our spirits is the Worry Habit.

Unlike the List Habit we explored in chapter eight, there is
no upside to the Worry Habit. Still, it's very easy to kick this
habit. All we have to do is learn to stay in the present moment.
But how are we to do that when we have so many issues about
our pasts and concerns about our futures? Well, we have to stop
worrying about them.

Worry and living in the present are integrally related.
Generally, when we are living in the present, not the past or
future, we find it easier not to worry.

The past cannot be changed. It can be overcome, and it can be forgiven, but it cannot change. We will explore forgiveness in the next two chapters.

The future has not happened yet; therefore, it is not real. Still, the future *can* be changed by our actions. Sometimes we think that justifies worrying about the future, but worry is not an action. It will not change the future. Only positive action in the present moment will affect the future. God alone knows exactly how our present actions will affect our futures, so, again, it is useless to worry about it.

THE TROUBLE WITH THE FUTURE

C.S. Lewis discussed this human inclination to worry about the future in his book, *The Screwtape Letters*. The premise of this book is a series of letters from one devil to another about how to "secure" the soul of a certain human being (the "patient") and get him condemned to hell. The older, wiser devil writing the letters advises his younger protégé to encourage the "patient" to think about the future. "In a word, the Future is, of all things, the thing *least like* eternity. It is the most completely temporal part of time—for the Past is frozen and no longer flows, and the Present is all lit up with eternal rays.... Hence nearly all vices are rooted in the Future."[2]

Kind of makes you want to stop worrying about the future, doesn't it? It is true, isn't it, that worry leads to sin. We worry that God will not provide for us, so we become dishonest in our finances or we neglect our families to spend time at the office. We worry that we will never be loved, so we get involved with the wrong people. We worry, and we give our soul's enemy a chance to move in on us.

Have you ever noticed that when you worry about the future, you cannot imagine God being there, solving the problem, bringing you through? Yet, time and time again, God does just that. Why don't we picture God's help when we worry? Because when we worry, we go ahead of God into a godless nonreality. God is not there in our worried imaginings; God is only in reality, in the eternal Present. When our future becomes the present, God will be there.

Most of our worries have to do with the future. Even when we dwell on the past, the context is usually how it will affect our future. We worry about how we will cope with life if such-and-such happens. What if one of the children gets hurt? What if I lose my job? What if someone dies? The answer to all these questions is, "Just fine *if* it happens, because God will be with me." If we insist on worrying, on going ahead of God into some dreadful scenario of the future, we are on our own. God cannot help us. God only gives us the strength to deal with present trials while we are actually experiencing them in reality.

· · • · ·

77

Even when we are not worrying about the future, we often try to escape the present because we are in pain. This may be healthy to a certain extent. Immersing oneself in a good book or movie or having a daydream session are acceptable ways to relieve stress. Still, the very best way to deal with present pain is to face it squarely. We must ask ourselves, especially when we are in mental anguish, "Am I okay right now, right this moment?" Often, we are. We can breathe, and we can do the deep breathing exercise in chapter three to prove it. We can ask God to help us shut down the disturbing images flitting through our minds. The great majority of things we fear never come to pass. The rest we are able to deal with because we are strong people, and God is always with us in our troubles.

Think of some of the trials you have gone through and how God helped you. Could you have imagined what really happened? Did you foresee the strength God gave you, the people who helped or the comfort you felt? Of course not. Our fears never seem to include God's provision for the moment. Their only subject matter is the terrible thing we may go through all by ourselves. They are not reality.

This present moment is where God is. C.S. Lewis wrote that the present "is all lit up with eternal rays." When and if troubles happen, the present is where we get the strength to deal with them. The present moment is the only one that touches eternity, the only reality.

The writer of Ecclesiastes says there is "a time to mourn, and a time to dance" (3:4). Do we miss the "dancing" times because we are busy worrying about the "mourning" times that may or may not happen? Let's not miss the dance because we are not paying attention to the present.

THE ANTIDOTE TO THE WORRY HABIT

I wrote, somewhat in jest, that the solution to worry is to stay in the present moment, and the trick to staying in the present moment is to stop worrying about the past or future.

There is a real antidote to the worry habit: gratitude. There is no room for both worry and gratitude in our hearts. Think of a game of musical chairs. Worry and Gratitude run around and around a chair until the music stops. Only one of them can sit in the chair when the music stops. For many of us, Worry usually wins and sits on the throne in our minds. We can change that. We can push Worry off and let Gratitude have a turn. When we begin to thank God for all the good things in our lives, worry seems a silly waste of time. Staying in the present moment is much easier.

In chapter ten we discussed work and said it can actually be enjoyable, that we can lose ourselves in "pleasant absorption and immersion." This happens when we let go of worry, immerse ourselves in the moment and have grateful hearts.

Let's make it our goal to be "present moment" people. Let's

practice gratitude, especially when worry tries to take over our hearts. Life will become simpler, easier and less cluttered.

ACTIVITIES

1. How much trouble do you have staying in the present moment? What is the usual subject matter of your worries? The past or the future? Talk with God about this. Ask for help staying in the present.

2. Begin a "gratitude list." Write down everything you can think of to thank God for: your health, your family, your home, your intellect. Most of all, thank God for his love and for creating you. Keep reading your list and adding to it as new things occur to you. Do you feel gratitude taking over the place worry used to occupy?

3. Make a God jar. Find a container you like and write notes to God to put inside. Tell God about your worries. Then put the slips of paper inside and leave them and your worries in God's hands.

NOTES

[1] Cameron, p. 54.

[2] C.S. Lewis, *The Screwtape Letters* (San Francisco: HarperSanFrancisco, 2001), p. 76.

CHAPTER THIRTEEN

FORGIVENESS 101

Forgive, if you have anything against any one;
so that your Father also who is in heaven may
forgive you your trespasses.
—Mark 11:25

THE RABBIT TRAP

The dog ran as I banged out of the house, making as much noise as I could. I stood on my deck, furious. It had happened again— someone had toured the house and, obviously, they were not going to buy.

You probably know what it is like to sell a house. During the fourteen months I tried to sell mine, people made appointments and never showed up. One actually laughed at something while I stood there. One couple assured me they wanted the house, but never showed for their appointment to make the offer. And one cold winter day, my dog Kelsey and I walked and walked outside for almost an hour while my agent showed the house. I was hopeful; it's always a good sign when people stay. Turns out, they were chatting about all the reasons they would never buy it.

The day I had my temper tantrum, I don't know who had just gone through the house. It didn't really matter. After a year of remodeling, repairing and cleaning frantically every time someone came, I was discouraged and angry at the whole world.

My anger focused on the one I was really bitter about: my ex-husband. Some of my issues had to do with the state the house was in when we divorced, but mostly I was angry at being single and having to deal with this alone. Whether my feelings were fair or not (I did insist on getting the house when we divorced), I had a lot of resentment after two years. Just then, an uncomfortable thought crossed my mind. Maybe God wanted me to deal with my anger before I started my new life in Arizona. The thought made me even angrier!

I intended to forgive. I tried to forgive. I thought I had many times. But my recurring anger was proof I had not. I always ended up in the same place: bitter, resentful, out of control and even irritated with God.

I sat down and tried to calm myself. God wanted to talk to me about it, I could tell. To be honest, I didn't want to hear what he had to say.

My eyes drifted over to a metal cage with a trapdoor stashed in a corner of the deck. This clever device was advertised as a merciful way to catch rabbits and relocate them to another area. The cage was covered with spiderwebs and dead leaves; no rabbit in our yard had ever been stupid enough to walk into it. The trap was a family joke and had become invisible in its corner, as clutter tends to do. But why was God pointing to the rabbit trap now?

God told me (very softly and carefully!) to open the trap door and let my ex-husband go free. An image came to mind:

That stupid rabbit trap with something inside. Yes, I *had* caught something, all right, but the trap was inside me, in my heart. It was a big, floppy-eared bunny—with my ex's face! God has such a sense of humor.

Today I can laugh at that image, but at the time I wasn't in the mood. I started to protest. How could I let it go? Various excuses ran through my mind, none of them making much sense.

The real reason I couldn't or wouldn't forgive was this: Without that little rabbit in my trap, I wouldn't have anyone to kick around or blame when things got tough. I could no longer blame my ex for not being able to sell the house. There *was* no one to blame. It was bad luck that the housing market was bad, that there were hundreds of average houses like mine for sale. There was really no one to blame, not myself, not God, not even my ex-husband.

I sat still for a few minutes, digesting this. God had spoken, and I knew what was expected. After crying a little, I gave in and let go. Mentally, I opened the trapdoor and let the little rabbit go free, to do whatever it would do. In my mind, I saw it bound off and disappear.

There was momentary grief, but immediately a sense of freedom flooded me. I had no idea the heavy burden I was carrying until that moment.

Forgiveness takes a long time. Often we do not want to forgive. We get something out of holding on. Other times we try and try, but realize we still have not forgiven someone. Our recurring anger or smoldering resentment proves we haven't let go.

Forgiveness is a lot like trying to quit tobacco or drugs—it may take a lot of failures before we succeed. Until we reach the final moment of letting go, we must continually move toward it. Before we forgive, we are handicapped, not able to do what we could if we were free. We spend a lot of time and energy better used elsewhere.

Nonforgiveness is a heavy spiritual load. It is clutter of the worst kind.

PARDON AND FORGIVENESS

If forgiveness is vitally important, and Jesus assures us it is, we had better learn something about it. The next chapter is about really difficult forgiveness. If you or a loved one have been permanently hurt or damaged by another's sin, that chapter is for you. For now, though, let's clear up a basic confusion about forgiveness and look at some techniques to help us.

Forgiveness is not pardon. Many of us do not know the difference. In fact, if we look up those terms in a dictionary, they seem interchangeable. *Pardon* is used as a secondary definition for *forgiveness* and vice versa. No wonder we believe forgiveness equals pardon. Why, then, would Jesus insist on forgiveness? In certain situations, letting the other person "off the hook"— pardoning them—is immoral. People who have committed crimes should be punished, shouldn't they? Spouses don't have to stay in abusive marriages, do they? Perhaps many crime victims and abused spouses do not press charges or do not divorce because they believe that is what forgiveness is. If so, we are confusing forgiveness with pardon.

According to Dr. Montague Brown, author of *The One-Minute Philosopher*, forgiveness is not the same as pardon. "Pardon is the external declaration that an offense will not be punished; forgiveness is the internal act of will that puts aside all hatred of the offender."[1]

In other words, forgiveness means we have been wronged, but we refuse to hate the wrongdoer. Forgiveness involves our attitude toward others. Pardon means a real wrong has been done, but it will go unpunished. Pardon is external. It is what is happening when women stay with husbands who beat them, when rape victims refuse to press charges, when parents repeatedly buy new cars and pay the fines for their reckless children. In many cases, pardon of this kind is irresponsible and often self-destructive, and in some cases harmful or dangerous to others.

In contrast, here is how forgiveness really works: The murderer, rapist, child molester goes to prison, but his victims refuse to hate him for the crime. The cheating wife is divorced after years of infidelity, but the wronged husband gets on with life and refuses to hate her. The drug-addicted child who steals from his family is turned out of the house, but his parents pray for him and are ready to help if he decides to go into rehabilitation. The toxic relative or neighbor is avoided, but her family and neighbors do not gossip about her. The rotten boss gets his notice as soon as the employee finds a better job, but the former employee does not spend his time obsessing about how he was treated.

We do not have to stay in a bad situation or allow ourselves to be abused in order to forgive. That would be a form of pardon. We do refuse to hate, gossip about, obsess over or brood about what others have done to us. We forgive and get on with life. God requires this of us. Forgiveness frees us of mental clutter.

Forgiveness is entirely different from pardon. Forgiveness says, "You did this, it was wrong, and I know it. I refuse to hate you for it or destroy myself inside because of it. I do, however, reserve the right to steer clear of you or press charges." Sometimes forgiveness is called "tough love." We forgive, but we do not allow the wrongdoer to victimize us anymore.

Forgiveness is something we do internally. It is a refusal to hate, resent or desire revenge. It is an act of the will, not a feeling.

Once we understand God is not asking us to *pardon* someone when we forgive, we can work on forgiveness.

How Do We Forgive?

We must first intend to forgive. We may not be able to do it yet.
It will take time, but we must be headed in that direction.
Dismissing our unforgiveness by saying, "I'll never forgive so-
and-so. She doesn't deserve it," is destructive to our spirits. To say
God does not understand the depth of our pain or the serious-
ness of the crime is a lie, and we know it. Jesus assures us we will
only be forgiven if we forgive. We cannot understand fully what
our rebellion and sins look like to God, but we know it took
Jesus' brutal death to set it right. If God says we have to forgive
in order to be forgiven, then we have to forgive.

After fully intending to forgive, we should examine ourselves and our inability to forgive. Whatever the other person
did, there is always something inside *us* that causes us to resent
this person more than any other. What is the issue here? Why
is this person so hard to forgive and not another who may be
equally guilty of hurting us? Sometimes, exploring the whole
relationship with a Christian psychologist, a member of the
clergy or a spiritual director will help us uncover what is really
going on under the surface. The object here is to heal and to
live free of spiritual clutter. We should not be afraid to ask for
help. Often we cannot do these things alone, and we should
not want to.

There are concrete steps we can take on the road to forgiveness. Visualization helps, like imagining a rabbit inside a trap and
setting it free. We may use a mental image to see ourselves free-
ing those who have hurt us, giving up our resentments. Letting
the captives in our minds go free means they no longer have to
answer to us, we no longer blame them for everything.

Mark Thibodeaux, a Jesuit priest and author of *God, I Have
Issues: 50 Ways to Pray No Matter How You Feel*, recommends
another visualization. Imagine three chairs, one for you, one for

85

the person you are trying to forgive and one for Jesus. Everyone sits down, and you begin talking to the person who wronged you. Say anything you want and need to say. Knowing Jesus is listening keeps the conversation civil. After you are done, let Jesus speak. What will he say about the situation?

I used this technique when I found myself very angry at someone we'll call Bob. I had my say, which felt very good. I made some very good points. When I was finished, I heard Jesus' small, still voice say, "Bob is scared." God never tells us the details of others' stories, but I concluded that Bob is aware of everything I brought up. He does not know what to do about the situation, which explains his behavior toward me. After this exercise, I had a different perspective. I was able to pray for Bob, not resent him. Forgiveness—letting him go—came easily after that.

Julia Cameron, author of *The Artist's Way*, recommends that her readers write three long-hand pages of "morning pages." These are rambling thoughts at the very beginning of the day, designed to get our creative juices going. I can testify that writing "morning pages" frees up the artist within each of us.

But "morning pages" are also helpful when trying to forgive someone. I found, quite by accident, this is a great way to work through forgiveness issues. It is similar to Father Mark's technique above, only on paper. It may take more than three pages to work through an issue, but write until you have gotten it out of your system. This is very important: Destroy those pages while visualizing letting go of the person you need to forgive. Do not under any circumstances keep reading them!

Like being cured of a physical disease, we must work to keep our spirits healthy. This means we do not tempt ourselves back into an attitude of nonforgiveness by reviewing past hurts. Letting go means the issue is settled. We do not revisit it; we do not infect ourselves again with the same resentments.

How do we know we have forgiven? When true and final forgiveness happens, we are able pray for the people who have hurt us. We desire God's best for them. We pray they receive the very things we pray for ourselves: Health in mind and spirit, internal peace, maturity, eternal life.

When we forgive, we are well on our way to freedom from spiritual clutter.

ACTIVITY

Examine your life. Is there anyone in your life whom you need to forgive? Take the steps necessary, starting today, to begin the process.

NOTES

[1] Montague Brown, *The One-Minute Philosopher: Quick Answers to Help You Banish Confusion, Resolve Controversies and Explain Yourself Better to Others* (Manchester, N.H.: Sophia Institute, 2001), pp. 46–47.

CHAPTER FOURTEEN

Advanced Forgiveness

Son, you are always with me, and all that is mine is yours.
But we had to celebrate and rejoice, because this brother
of yours was dead and has come to life; he was
lost and has been found.
—Luke 15:31–32

Years ago I was telling a friend about the death of a family member, a man who had refused to believe all his life and reconciled with God shortly before his death. We were rejoicing that he had died a peaceful, happy death and was now in heaven.

A woman standing nearby, a friend of my friend, interrupted us. Deathbed confessions, she protested, were totally unfair to those who had served God all their lives. It turns out this woman had an alcoholic father who had abused her throughout childhood. He had repented late in life, made a "deathbed confession," and presumably walked right into heaven. His daughter was not happy about what she felt was an injustice on God's part. "He ruined my life," she said. She did not have to go into details. Difficulty choosing a marriage partner, parenting children and trusting anyone are the usual results of such a childhood.

This chapter is about forgiving those who have hurt us so deeply that we could say they have "ruined" our lives. God does not allow anyone to actually destroy our spirits, but people do cause lifelong pain and grief. The parents who have lost a child to a drunk driver, the victim of childhood abuse or rape, the abandoned spouse, rightfully feel their lives will never be the same. This is not easy reading for those dealing with present difficulties because of someone else's sin. To be honest, I would rather not be writing this chapter, but I feel God wants me to. Too many of us are not only carrying the pain of our pasts, but also the pain of not being able to forgive.

There are people who really do not *seem* to deserve any type of forgiveness, people who have hurt us so badly, it seems all bets are off. Jesus could not have been talking about them when he said we have to forgive to be forgiven, right? No matter how wicked some people's actions, they come under the same umbrella—forgiveness is required. This includes the murderer, the rapist, the cheating spouse, the alcoholic, the abusive parent, the sexual predator.

It is hard to recover from the anguish others have inflicted upon us. It may take a lifetime to let go. Sin always has consequences. Unfortunately, those consequences also fall on family members of the sinner and other innocent bystanders. Yes, our lives can be adversely affected by the sins of others. Still, we cannot say these people have *ruined* us. There is always hope of healing in Christ. Even if we are wounded and unable to trust, God still reaches us. Part of our healing is letting go of and forgiving those who have damaged us. In fact, it is probably the biggest part.

Two of Jesus' parables give us a clear picture of forgiveness from God's point of view. The Prodigal Son (Luke 15:11–32) is welcomed back and reinstated into the family after leaving his family and squandering his inheritance on selfish living. In that parable the boy's father (our heavenly Father) waits anxiously for his child to come to his senses. The older son, reluctant to forgive, is scolded. Notice, however, it does not say the younger son got *another* inheritance to squander! He was forgiven, not pardoned or enabled!

In another parable, the Workers in the Vineyard (Matthew 20:1–16), a group of workers arrive late, work only an hour and get the same wage as those who worked all day. This seems to be the issue bothering the woman at the beginning of this chapter. Are there no consequences to sin if we "make up" to God on our deathbeds? Does it pay to be faithful all our lives, or should we just "live it up" and repent at the very end?

Aside from the obvious fact many of us will not have time at the end to repent if we live sinful lives, Scripture is full of warnings about the wages of sin. In telling these parables, Jesus is not saying there are no consequences to sin. Yes, the prodigal *will* be welcomed home if he or she is willing to return to God. Those who come to faith late in life *will* receive the same reward as those who were faithful much longer. There are still consequences to our actions.

All of us are becoming *someone*. God created us to become sons and daughters, but we do not have to fulfill our destiny. We are free to choose who we will become. God sends us into this world with an armful of gifts and talents. Every choice we make to use them or not to use them moves us toward the persons we ultimately become. For people of faith, many of our choices, maybe most of them, have nothing to do with sin. We make choices between one good thing and another all our lives. We choose one thing over another, and we become somebody different through each choice.

What are the consequences of a lifetime of bad choices? What if we choose addiction, abuse of others, self-indulgence? We become someone God never intended us to be. We become wounded, crippled, twisted in spirit. The deep sinner never lives a great life, makes a "deathbed confession" and walks merrily into heaven, happy to have bypassed all the disciplines of a faith-filled life. No, if she makes it at all (and it is very difficult to desire eternal life after a lifetime of bad choices), it is as a bedraggled, sorry child who sincerely regrets every moment of her earthly life.

Be certain about this: There are consequences to every action. Those who waste this life in selfishness and wake up to their true situation shortly before death are not to be envied. They have not lived a fun life. None of us know what anguish they go through—the self-hatred, the fear, the chaos—all their lives. If they, like the Prodigal Son, wake up and decide to throw themselves on God's mercy, we should be ecstatically happy for them. If they have hurt us along the way—and they will have hurt *everybody* in their paths—we must be content to leave them in Jesus' hands. We must be willing to welcome them back to the family of God.

God does not wish any sinner to perish (2 Peter 3:9; 1 Timothy 2:4). Neither should we.

What about us "workers in the vineyard" who try to be faithful all our lives? We, too, have "labored all day in the hot sun." Does God really give everyone the same reward in the end? If this thought disturbs us, we must remember God will give us more than we could possibly ask for or imagine in heaven. What more could we ask than eternal joy and happiness? If those who "worked" less than us on earth get the same, what difference could it possibly make?

The kingdom of God is not an exclusive club we earn our way into, something we "good people" get to enjoy. Christians today, especially well-off Christians today, may be confused about the kingdom. We become immersed in the good things of this world. We work hard to acquire the nice house in the suburbs, the padded bank account, the college education for our kids, the comfortable retirement. Sometimes we actually believe we have earned all this because we worked for it. We may forget that earthly success is often a happy accident of birth, something we should never claim credit for. We could just as well have been born in totally different circumstances.

When we apply this kind of thinking to spiritual matters, we may think our goodness is something to be proud of, that heaven is full of "our kind" of people who have earned eternal happiness. Jesus makes it clear that this is not true. Heaven is not a country club.

Just as there are people who will not eat today without help, through no fault of their own, there are people who will never make it to heaven without a great deal of help. Judging them is not our business. Our role is to help whomever we can without criticism.

When the refugees from Hurricane Katrina straggled out of New Orleans in 2005, cold, hungry and dirty, no one scolded them for being wet and smelly. No, we rejoiced they had survived. We gave them hot food, clothing, showers and warm beds. We found them jobs and new houses, so they could start their lives over again.

I believe heaven is the same. We are all refugees. No one is going to scold us when we arrive at the eternal city bedraggled, hungry and smelly—and we will be. Everyone already in heaven, especially God, will welcome us and rejoice in our arrival. And if we happen to notice other refugees along the way who treated us badly in the past but are now headed back to God, we should be happy to put our arms around them and help them get home.

QUESTIONS FOR REFLECTION

1. Is there anyone you find it hard to forgive because of the hurt he or she inflicted upon you?
2. Do Jesus' parables of the Prodigal Son and the Workers in the Vineyard help you gain a perspective on forgiving this person?

ACTIVITIES

1. Pray for the person or persons you are trying to forgive. Try to envision them wounded and needing all the help God can give them to achieve eternity. Ask God to help you.
2. If you have not already done so, find a wise counselor or objective person to whom you can discuss your feelings about the person you are trying to forgive.

CHAPTER FIFTEEN

WAITING FOR GOD

Waiting seems to be a kind of acted-out prayer that
is required more often and honored more often....
[the waiting prayer] is an astonishing experience in
poised expectancy.
—Catherine Marshall, *Adventures in Prayer*[1]

"I was supposed to be there by now," I complained.

The long wait to sell my house in Ohio was straining my finances. What bothered me more was it had upset all my plans and expectations. I planned to move in the summer of 2003; I expected to have enough money left over from the sale of the house to take a few months off to write before I found a job. I felt God was blessing this move. Why was this happening?

I had visited Arizona for Christmas in 2003 and arranged to look at houses with a real estate agent, never expecting I would find the perfect house. It was a fixer-upper in my price range at the foot of the Superstition Mountains, an area I have visited and loved for thirty years. I believed then and still believe God saved this house for me. It came on the market the day before I toured the area. Several people were thinking of buying it, but I put in the first bid, completely unaware of all the drama associated with it. Later I learned that I bought the last affordable house in the neighborhood. Buying it was like winning the lottery.

Knowing that, I found it inexplicable that I could not sell my house in Ohio. If God was behind all this, if I was supposed to buy the house in Arizona, shouldn't the house in Ohio have sold immediately? That's how I would do things if I were God! But no, winter dragged on, then spring and summer. No offers. I was getting short of money. "What in the world are you doing?" I asked God.

Waiting for something to happen—big or small—can be excruciating. Believing it is God's will does not help. A well-meaning friend told me "God is never late, but seldom early." It felt as though God was already very late.

During the wait to sell my house, I learned a few things. First and foremost, God is God, and I'm not. God's timetable and mine are not necessarily the same. Also, my financial problems, although of concern to God, were not fatal. I survived. I learned we are never supposed to be anywhere but where we are. We may hope we could be elsewhere. We may be disappointed not to be there. But we are not *supposed* to be there.

How to Wait for God

The "prayer of waiting" does not involve dictating a timetable to God, getting angry or doubting our choices. All these things are spiritual clutter and keep us from seeing the true beauty and sheer genius of what God is doing. Waiting is an exercise in patience and in trust. We may believe things should happen a certain way, but God knows better.

How do we wait for God, especially when delays sometimes strain our budgets and our nerves?

First, we must trust. We cannot see what God sees. If I had waited to buy the house in Arizona until I sold the one in Ohio, someone else would have bought it. Even if it had stayed on the market, I could not have afforded it. The housing market in Arizona went crazy soon after I bought the house. God could have spelled this all out for me, but seldom does. Trust and faith involve not knowing everything.

What Should We Do While We Wait?

We should do those things we would do if we were absolutely sure the event was going to take place. The person who is waiting to move should pack. The person waiting for a job should keep going to interviews. The parent waiting for a grown child to find his way should keep loving and supporting the child. God *is* working while we wait. All will be well. It is not a matter of denial; it is a matter of hope and expectation.

Oswald Chambers, author of *My Utmost for His Highest*, calls this *tenacity*. Spiritual tenacity, Chambers writes, means more than hanging onto God because we are afraid to let go. When we wait for God, we do not sit around doing nothing. We "work deliberately on the certainty that God is not going to be worsted."[2] I had difficulty with that; I spent a lot of time getting upset instead of believing and packing. I should have worked faster, because when God acts, there is little advance notice.

What Is God Doing While We Wait?

While we are waiting for God, we should notice what God is doing around us. What is happening that could not possibly have happened if our prayers had been answered sooner? I have a list of the things God did during those fourteen months I waited for the house to sell. It was one of the most miraculous periods in my life. I took a mission trip to El Salvador, did an important book-editing project and strengthened relationships with three key people in my life before I moved away from them. Shortly after having a dream in which I was driving to Arizona with a big yellow dog on the seat next to me, my neighbor found my dog Kelsey and gave her to me. None of these things would have happened if I had moved earlier.

Noticing what God is doing while we are waiting for this life-changing, "I'll be okay when _____ happens" event is instructional. While we may be counting the days, tapping our feet and biting our nails, God is working all around us. Do we notice, or do we become more anxious as the days, weeks and months go by?

One of the things we may want to do while waiting for God is to avoid people who insist on talking about our troubles but are not supportive. For many people our waiting for God makes them uncomfortable, so they say things. "Isn't that house sold, yet?" "Are you pregnant yet?" "Haven't you found a job?" "Don't you ever plan to get married?" Questions like this hurt us and shake our faith. These interrogations may even make us feel foolish for trusting God. If there are people who make us feel bad about waiting for God, we should avoid them. This is called self-protection.

Trusting God requires a certain amount of passivity. We work, knowing and believing God will come through for us. We try not to take matters into our own hands entirely. This is a tough call. We cannot be totally passive and do nothing. We have to "work deliberately," as Oswald Chambers says, but we cannot get ahead of God. We must refuse to do things in a state of panic. We must not try to make things happen. Remember what we said in chapter eleven: Life is a cooperative partnership between God and us.

GOD IS ON OUR SIDE!

Waiting is a sign the time is not right. It does not mean God has abandoned us. God does not play games with us, does not torture us by making us desire things we cannot have. Remember God has to wait also. God may be waiting for the future buyer of your home to make a decision. The future employer may need to get her act together. The wayward child may need to grow up a bit. Just as God does not push or rush us, he does not rush others. God does a lot more waiting than we realize.

Expectancy is the key to waiting for God. What we wait for *will* come to pass. Are we waiting expectantly for it? The best part of waiting is seeing how God fulfills our dreams and watching the miracle unfold in our lives.

QUESTIONS FOR REFLECTION

1. Are you waiting for something important to happen? Do you feel things are going too slowly? What problems are you experiencing?

2. Have you experienced this type of waiting before? In the end, what happened? Did you see God's hand in the resolution of the matter?

ACTIVITY

Make a list of all the good things that have happened in your life while waiting for something else. Are you surprised at how many good things were happening during that period of your life?

NOTES
[1] Catherine Marshall, *Adventures in Prayer* (New York: Ballantine, 1975), p. 51.
[2] Oswald Chambers, *My Utmost for His Highest: Selections for the Year* (New York: Dodd, Mead and Company, 1935), p. 53.

SECTION FIVE

GOD WITHOUT CLUTTER: PRACTICING FOR ETERNITY

We are beginning a whole new section—the last in this book. We have talked about taking care of ourselves, clearing the clutter out of our physical environment, working in new ways and overcoming mental and spiritual "clutter" that keeps us from growing.

Once we have cleared out as much of our clutter as we can, what do we do with ourselves? From this point on, we no longer talk much about clutter. This section deals with those positive and enjoyable things God wants us to do during our sojourn on earth. These things are the heart of our spiritual lives.

We begin with prayer and make it easier to do on a daily basis. We learn how to keep the Sabbath, thus experiencing eternity every week. Next, we discuss community. We are going to be spending eternity together. Our earthly life is practice for this. Finally, we discuss creativity, which is the sign of God's life in us and proof we are made in God's image.

CHAPTER SIXTEEN

PRAYER: IT'S EASIER THAN YOU THINK

> When it comes to our relationship with God, God
> always takes the initiative. This means we don't have
> to worry about asking God to the dance; God is
> already on the phone asking us!
> —Melannie Svoboda, *Rummaging for God*[1]

What a wonderful image of prayer—God calling me on the phone to ask me to the dance.

I love this image for two reasons. First, I was awkward, shy and insecure as a teen. Any time a boy called me to ask for a date was a thrill. Second, God's calling us on the phone is a good image.

Prayer has this built-in difficulty: Although God is as near to us as our heartbeat, the relationship is like a long-distance relationship on earth. We cannot see God face to face. Much of what we know of God we know through faith, not through seeing or hanging out together.

How do loved ones sustain long-distance relationships? How do couples who are separated, parents whose children and grandchildren live in different states or countries, friends who live far away, keep the relationship fresh?

The answer is *intention*. If we are separated from loved ones, we schedule times to talk on the phone or over the Internet. We respond when we miss a call by returning the call promptly. We do not let too much time go by between visits. We do not call only when there is big news; we call just to say, "Hi. I love you." We also keep reminders of distant loved ones all around us. We have photos all around the house of children, grandchildren, parents, friends. We keep their letters and save their e-mails.

LIVING WITH INTENTION

All these things apply to God as well. Like all relationships, the one with God requires intention, regularity and reminders. We make staying in touch with God a priority. We schedule time to meet God daily. We remind ourselves of God by keeping religious articles and Scripture verses around the house. We leave our Bibles and prayer books out so we will remember to read them. God has given us the Scriptures as a type of "love letter" that we must read over and over. Best of all, Jesus gave us the Eucharist to keep the relationship fresh and vital: "Do this in remembrance of me."

We get so busy, though. How do we give prayer its proper place in our lives when our days are so full already?

Have you ever heard someone say, "My work is my prayer"? People who work for religious organizations or social causes sometimes say this. Like the rest of us, they are "doing" constantly. We cannot substitute work for our relationship with God, no matter how sacred the work.

"My work is my prayer" is like saying "my work is my meal." Anyone who works to the point of skipping their prayers is going to be in the same type of trouble as those who skip meals. We eat so we *can* work. In the same way, we pray so we can work.

Once we get this connection, we see there are rules about prayer, and these rules are similar to those about eating. Food must be eaten regularly and is essential to life. We need to do some planning in order to eat well. We need variety in our diet, and we need companions with which to eat. Yes, we also eat alone, but life would not be worth living if we never had companions. Eating together is one of our greatest human pleasures.

Prayer, too, must be done regularly and is essential. Planning is required. Our prayer lives should have interesting variety. And life would not be worth living if we always had to pray alone. Praying with companions, our brothers and sisters in the Body of Christ, is as essential in prayer as in eating. There must also be the private component of prayer. Our daily, private talks with God are essential. But we bring the fruits of private prayer to our companions when we gather with them.

Planning Prayer

How does one plan a prayer time? This is different for each of us, but planning involves setting aside the time for an activity and having supplies on hand to do it. When we plan our meals, we decide what time we want to eat, and we have the ingredients to make a meal.

What happens when we do not plan our prayer? About the same thing that happens when we do not plan our meals. We end up not praying at all until there is some emergency. We let ourselves become tense and stressed out, then we turn to God. When we skip a meal, our blood sugar bottoms out, we get crabby and confused, and we grab the easiest thing, usually fast food or sweets. When we skip prayer, we also get crabby and confused. Life becomes harder, we become spiritually unhealthy.

Take time every day (at least fifteen to twenty minutes) to meet with God. Devote that time to conversing with God. This is just a beginning. Done regularly, it will lead to an easy, daylong, comfortable relationship with God, a continuous "conversation" with the Creator.

In addition to that daily appointment, begin the day with your good-morning journal to remind you of God's presence. Chat with God on the drive to work. Have a cup of coffee together. Invite God to share your meals. You never have to eat alone. Chat with God while you eat, while you drive, while you brush your teeth, while you work out at the gym.

"Prayer time" should become as ingrained as "mealtime." Most of us, even if we skip meals once in a while, know when it is mealtime. We think of it automatically. We feel hungry. We know we missed something. In the same way, we must listen to our spirits. Our hearts will tell us when it is time to pray, when we are hungry for God.

During our prayer times, we should not limit ourselves to traditional prayers or even Scripture reading. We should not do all the talking. God desires a relationship with us. Relationships involve two-way communication. We would not talk to our friends the way we usually talk to God. Wouldn't it be strange if a friend asked us to lunch, read a message to us someone else had written for them, then got up and walked away? Isn't that what we often do to God? Using traditional prayers—the rosary, the Psalms or the Divine Office—during prayer is good. But we must also be quiet and listen. We should include time for dialogue. We should "hang out" with God, talk with God like a friend. Prayer is not hard. It is talking. We do it all the time.

Sometimes we make prayer difficult. Maybe we have been out of touch for a long time; maybe we believe we are not allowed to be too familiar with God. We tend to clutter up our relationship with God, just as we do in other areas of life. Let's not complicate prayer to the point where we are reluctant to talk to God, believing he must be disappointed in us or angry at our inattentiveness.

Preparing to Pray

Do we feel we have to do things for God or clean up our act before we are allowed to talk freely? Do we feel we must explain where we've been, why we haven't been in touch? Do we feel we owe God an apology before we can talk to him? None of this is necessary. God knows where we have been and what we have been doing. God knows why we think we are too busy to pray. We do not have to impress God. We cannot pretend to be someone we are not. All we need do is ask God to help us to be more faithful. We do not have to "clean up our act" for God.

Relationship clutter is anything we think we have to do prior to getting into the good parts of the relationship: the sharing and love and enjoyment of the other person's company. This is what God desires: to share our lives, to enjoy and love us. God does not require "preliminaries." God is not disappointed in us. God does not have "issues." God does not scold us about our lack of attention or faith before giving us a hug. We do these things to one other. God does not.

"God without clutter" means God is the one who draws us out, who approaches us first, who asks us to the dance first. Just as clearing out the clutter in a room calls attention to its real beauty, God will help us clear out our inner clutter so the relationship with our Creator is free, easy and enjoyable.

So let's begin today. This is the first step in "practicing for eternity." It should be enjoyable. God is fun! Spend time with God every day, get to know one another, keep it simple and easy. Prayer is as easy as hanging out with a friend, as simple as preparing our meals and eating them.

ACTIVITIES

Do some planning in order to meet with God daily. Here are some suggestions about how to find time to meet with God:

- Choose a fifteen- to twenty-minute block of time that works for you: Many people choose a time at the beginning of the day, perhaps when everyone else is still in bed or after they have left for the day.
- Find time to pray throughout the day—perhaps in your car or on the bus on your way to and from work or when you are exercising or out for a walk.
- At work close your office door and take a few minutes or use some of your lunchtime to meet with God.
- In the evening spend a few minutes before bed to thank God for the day and place any cares in God's keeping for the night.

Special Notes About Prayer Time:

- Consider your physical surroundings when you pray. Do you have a place where you will be left alone, where there are no noises, conversations or distractions?
- Can you go outside or stop somewhere (in a church or a park or a scenic place) on the way to or from work?
- Consider any supplies you will need for prayer. My suggestions are a Bible, any prayer books you like, a notebook and a pen. Put all these items in a bag and park it near your chosen place to pray or near the door if you prefer to go somewhere else to pray.

NOTE

[1]Melannie Svoboda, *Rummaging for God: Seeking the Holy in Every Nook and Cranny* (Mystic, Conn.: Twenty-Third, 1999), p. 35.

CHAPTER SEVENTEEN

SABBATH REST

[T]hose who enter God's rest also cease from their labors as
God did from his. Let us therefore make every effort to
enter that rest.
—Hebrews 4:10–11

What would you do if you had a whole day to do as you pleased,
if you had no obligations, no projects, no one to work for, cook
for, clean up after? How would you spend the day? Take a few
minutes to think about it. In fact, grab a piece of paper right now
and write down whatever comes to mind.

Would you visit a friend? Would you play ball with a child
or grandchild? Would you reevaluate your life, do some deep
thinking about things? Would you curl up in bed with a good
book and a box of bonbons? Would you collapse from sheer
exhaustion?

Let me introduce a friend many of us have forgotten or have
never met: the Sabbath. This day, a gift of God, is a day to do

nothing, a day of no obligations. If this sounds wonderful, if you cannot remember the last time you did nothing, you are missing out. God has given us permission. In fact, God commands us to keep the Sabbath every week.

What Is the Sabbath?

Christians have long equated the Sabbath with going to church on Sundays. What do we do the rest of the day after services are over? Are Sundays spent rushing to church, eating out or cooking a big Sunday dinner at home, shopping, watching sports on TV and getting chores done? How restful is that? This is not the Sabbath.

In the Jewish tradition the Sabbath is a day of total rest and rejuvenation, not another day of "doing." It is a day for "being."

Our culture does not respect the Sabbath. With the god of productivity taking the place of the God of Abraham, Isaac and Jacob, the idea of taking a whole day off to do nothing seems ridiculous. This is not what we do today. We must move fast to keep up. Information must be assimilated. Both parents work in most households. Corporate downsizing means many of us are doing the jobs of two or three. Our workweek is filled with obligations. We are allowed our weekends to get our shopping done, clean the house, pay bills and spend some time with family. On Monday we get back in the harness again. We cannot possibly take a day off.

If our culture disrespects the Sabbath, it is not the first. The Egyptians and Romans were notoriously intolerant of the Jewish people's observance of Sabbath. Leo Trepp, author of *A History of the Jewish Experience,* refers to Juvenal's, the Roman writer, satire of the Jewish people who "turned lazy, taking no part in the tasks and duties of life" every seven days.[1] Many Romans regarded the Jews' taking a *whole* day off *every* week as a sign of their disloyalty and laziness. Their sentiments would be popular among some employers today.

Why do we so blithely disobey one of the Ten Commandments today? Most of us would never dream of committing murder or adultery; we are even embarrassed to take the Lord's name in vain. But we never protest our culture's insistence on work, work, work—sixteen hours a day, seven days a week.

PRINCES AND PRINCESSES FOR A DAY

Trepp writes that the Sabbath transformed the Jewish people from "hunted and persecuted outcasts of history into princes— for twenty-four hours, once every week."[2] This irritated whatever group was currently enslaving them. Slavemasters, whether in the ancient world or today, know that people who take one day out of seven to rest, pray and be at peace are really free, no matter how poor or downtrodden the other six days of the week.

Any power that makes slaves out of people cannot tolerate being ignored. The Jewish people's insistence on observing their laws, especially the Sabbath, has been the focal point of various persecutions through history. It would appear the Sabbath is countercultural in every age.

The Sabbath is the most important feast day in Judaism. Even if it falls on the same day as feasts like Passover, it takes precedence. There are a lot of "thou shalt nots" associated with Sabbath, for a good reason. In order to become who we *are*, we must stop doing what we normally *do*. The Sabbath is a divine awareness of time. Nature cannot distinguish one day from another; a cow does not know when it is Sabbath. Therefore, if we are to observe the Sabbath, we must be intentional about it. We must STOP—stop working, cooking, sewing, shopping, eating out, running around. This leaves the Sabbath free— frighteningly free to most of us—to do as we please and to be our true selves. This is why God insists on it and why our culture detests it.

When I first learned about the Jewish Sabbath, I was fascinated. I thought it was impossible, but I was fascinated. At the
time I was working part-time, attending college full-time (an
hour away from home) and interning at a parish. Working,
attending classes, doing my internship hours and traveling took
fifty-five hours a week. This was before I ate, slept or did any
studying. Take one day off every week? Right!

But a strange thing happened: God urged me to give the
Sabbath a try. In fact, God insisted I give the Sabbath a try.
Apparently, my schedule did not impress God. So I started taking a few hours off on Saturdays (Sunday was a work day for
me). I was restless and wanted the time to be over, as though it
were jail time. I had so many things to do.

God kept up the pressure, wanting me to forget all my duties
for one day. I learned new ways to do my work so I could
observe the Sabbath fully. I typed up first drafts of college papers
for the week ahead on Friday nights. Sometimes it took until
2:00 AM, but I got everything on paper, turned off the computer
and closed the door to my office. I spent Saturdays doing nothing, in essence, observing the Sabbath. I took a lot of naps. I read
fun, noncollege books. I ate and relaxed. On Sunday nights I finished my assignments, got a good night's sleep and began the
new week refreshed and energized. I took a whole day off every
week, but I got more done than I ever managed before. I was
hooked.

I still keep the Sabbath. It has been four years. I look forward
to it the way most of us look forward to a vacation at a tropical
resort. This command of God is a pleasant experience. My health
has improved so much, I can count on one hand the number of
days I have been sick enough to take to my bed.

These days my Sabbaths are not as quiet as they were when
I was in college. I was with people all the time then. My Sabbath

was a time to withdraw. Now I work at home, so my Sabbaths are more social. But I would not give up my special day anymore than I would give up eating and breathing!

Our society today encourages us to run after many things, to keep busy, to be productive. We are unbalanced, stressed-out and often bewildered. Into all this confusion, the Sabbath is more relevant than ever. "STOP!" God tells us. "Be still and know that I am God." The very fact that the Sabbath is less and less revered today by people of all religions is proof of how far we have drifted from God and our true selves. The rush to get things done is not what life is all about.

In the middle of all our busy-ness, the Sabbath beckons us to let it all go one day out of seven. Rediscovering the Sabbath may be the only way to save ourselves from this age. During the Sabbath we become free people again. We become truly human. We remember we have a destiny other than slavery to the corporate, consumer, productivity gods. We experience God's joy. We touch eternity.

God's command to observe the Sabbath and keep it holy is a pleasure and a privilege. It is a gift from our God who knows this world will make us work and work until we drop dead. The Sabbath is a gift for every man, woman and child. We use it to become a gift to others: to listen, to be available, to play, to show others how to really live.

How Do We Begin to Observe the Sabbath?

How do we begin observing the Sabbath, given what our schedules look like these days? We first have to experience Sabbath in order to appreciate it. We begin with an intention. We ask God to help us. We learn as we do it.

The thought of giving up one day a week may make us break out in a sweat. Most of us have enough work to keep us busy ten days a week. But those who tithe, who give 10 percent of their income to God, know their money somehow stretches and they are in better financial shape than ever. The Sabbath works the same way. It expands time, just as tithing expands income. Schedules loosen, we get the important things done, we learn to relax. How does God do it? Maybe we unconsciously reset our priorities. Maybe it is simply the fruit of obedience. It works. Whatever we give to God, we get back multiplied a thousand times!

There are certain things we do not do on the Sabbath. It is important to follow the rules so we enjoy the day fully.

Based on the Jewish principle that one does not make others work on the Sabbath, we avoid all forms of consumerism this day. We do not shop, eat out or hire others to work around our houses on the Sabbath. These activities are part of the usual workweek; we are taking the day off. All meal preparations for the day are done before the Sabbath begins. Yes, even moms get to relax this day. Everyone helps themselves to previously prepared food, and the dishes are left in the sink for one day.

On the Sabbath we do not force ourselves to do anything. We may read, journal, soak in the tub, take a walk, listen to music, hang out with friends and family. We relax and de-stress. Most of all, we commune with God, with creation, with ourselves.

The Sabbath is about trust. It is about reliance upon a God who does not require us to be productive before loving us. There is no striving, no working for our keep, no worrying about being worthy. The Sabbath is a taste of heaven, and it prepares us to live in eternity, because eternity is one long Sabbath. Abraham Joshua Heschel, author of *The Sabbath,* wrote, "Unless one learns how to relish the taste of Sabbath while still in this world...one will be unable to enjoy the taste of eternity in the world to come."[3]

If we begin to observe the Sabbath, we will find ourselves calmer, healthier and happier. We will be in touch with God, ourselves and those around us. The greatest benefit to observing the Sabbath faithfully is our becoming "Sabbath people" who understand that the Sabbath permeates the whole week with calm, peace and order, no matter what our circumstances.

QUESTIONS FOR REFLECTION

1. What do you normally do on your Sabbath? Do you work around the house? Do you do work brought from the office? Do you study?
2. Is there a way to rearrange your schedule to free up entirely one day of work?

ACTIVITIES

1. Begin to seriously plan to spend a Sabbath every week with God and with yourself. What will you have to do to make sure this day is uninterrupted by the world's demands?
2. Once you begin to take a Sabbath every week, evaluate what has happened in your life. Do you work more efficiently during the week? Are you more relaxed and patient? Do you look forward to the Sabbath?

NOTES

[1] Leo Trepp, *A History of the Jewish Experience: External Faith, Eternal People* (West Orange, N.J.: Behrman House, 1962), p. 75.

[2] Trepp, p. 1.

[3] Abraham Joshua Heschel, *The Sabbath* (New York: Farrar, Straus and Giroux, 1979), p. 74.

CHAPTER EIGHTEEN

COMMUNITY

> When I lived in Amsterdam, a common topic of discussion
> among colleagues was the loneliness of the city.... What we
> needed was some hot-climate spontaneous relationship and
> a little less cold-climate structured privacy.
> —Sarah A. Lanier, *Foreign to Familiar*[1]

What do you imagine heaven is like? Most of us imagine heaven
to be like the best times we have on earth. Holidays at
Grandma's, family reunions, weddings. In biblical times wedding
feasts were the ultimate good time and went on for days. It is not
surprising that the Bible's image of heaven is a wedding feast.

I picture heaven as one gigantic party with eating, drinking,
dancing and a big dessert table with lots of chocolate. I will see
those people I have been missing since they left this earth, but I
will also meet lots of people I never got to meet here: three of
my grandparents, certain favorite saints and C.S. Lewis.

Aren't the best times of our lives those wonderful family
gatherings—the weddings, parties, reunions? The truth is that

the Body of Christ is our eternal family. From everything I read in the Bible, heaven is more like a communal feast than anything else.

Like observing the Sabbath, community is very important in heaven. We should be practicing. Again, our culture does not help us. We are becoming increasingly isolated. Any culture emphasizing productivity cannot allow us to spend much time socializing, much less practicing the type of fellowship found in heaven.

Sarah Lanier, author of *Foreign to Familiar: A Guide to Understanding Hot- and Cold-Climate Cultures,* has lived all over the world. She has experienced cultures in the Middle East, Europe, South America, Africa and Asia. She divides cultures into two broad categories: "hot-climate" and "cold-climate" cultures. Hot-climate cultures are communal, group-oriented, inclusive and spontaneous. Cold-climate cultures are more individualistic, privacy-oriented and interested in structure and productivity. Each type of culture has its strengths and weakness; neither is intrinsically "good" or "bad." However, our culture's overemphasis on work, structure and privacy has led to isolationism. We have much to learn from our "hot-climate" neighbors.

Lanier writes about a bus trip she took in Thailand. An experienced traveler, she packed a lunch for the trip, along with some extra food. At noon she unpacked her lunch and began passing out her extra fruit and cookies to the other passengers. Soon others did the same, and food was being shared with everyone on the bus. There were, undoubtedly, people there who had nothing, but they were included in the meal with no embarrassment to themselves.

"Because everyone shared, we were not aware of the 'haves and the have nots.'" Lanier writes. "They were covered by the community. The inclusion value of hot-climate cultures means that no one is left out, no one is lonely."[2] For those of us who are Christians and concerned about the poor among us, what an easy solution to the whole problem. Share. Make sure we always have a little extra with us. Share on the bus or with those immediately around us. What if everyone did that everywhere?

Another trait of "cold-climate" cultures is loneliness. Although every human being experiences this at times, the crushing loneliness many experience in our culture is not universal. In "hot climates" this is not allowed. After traveling to Chile, Lanier wrote she "never met a lonely person. It was almost impossible to be lonely. People were always dropping in, settling into your kitchen while you cooked, and chatting away. If you wanted to be with people, you just walked out your door and started visiting."[3]

I experienced the same thing when I visited El Salvador in 2004. The people of the villages we visited were incredibly poor—and the happiest people I have ever met. They were always willing to stop and talk. Like us, they worked hard, but there was always time for other people. The poorest family in the village had a full crib of corn shared by their neighbors. Those same neighbors were taking turns cooking for the family because the wife was in the hospital. The old lady with mental problems who wandered into a service was calmed down and others made room for her in their pew. The children had their own happy community, running around, making noise and enjoying being kids, while their elders smiled at them and scolded them when they got too rambunctious. In spite of the language barrier, I felt right at home. When I got back, I was homesick for El Salvador.

My friend, Barbara, lived in an "intentional" Christian community from 1973 to 1983. Her community of sixty or more members was part of a network of Christian cell groups in western Pennsylvania founded by Pete Steen, a Christian Reformed teacher and evangelist. Steen spoke at Christian colleges, urging young people to serve Jesus by dedicating every aspect of their lives to him. People in the communities lived together or in the same houses or neighborhood, met for prayer and study, built and remodeled each other's houses, raised crops and gave them to the poor. Although the community formally disbanded over twenty years ago, the ties formed during that period continue today. Barbara told me that most of them feel much closer to one another than to members of their churches or even family members.

Those ten years "in community" have changed Barbara permanently. She still looks at the world in a different way, which sometimes startles people who know her. Barbara thinks nothing of dropping in to help a friend put new shelf paper in her kitchen or paint a room. We have cleared out her basement together, and she packed up my kitchen when I moved. Barbara is a "hot-climate" person to the core.

In our isolationist culture, it seems the only time we "live in community" is when there is a tragedy. Then, we forget our conditioning and become "hot-climate" people. Family, friends and neighbors converge upon the troubled family with food, comfort and company. This means we know how to live in community. Why can't we do this at other times?

Anne Lamott, author of *Traveling Mercies,* writes about friends whose daughter has cystic fibrosis. During the winter or after a visitor with a cold comes to their house, their little girl may spend weeks at a time in the hospital with pneumonia. Lamott writes, "I saw that the people who loved them could build a marvelous barn of sorts around the family." So they did. Friends simply showed up. They cleaned, took care of the children, took the dog for walks. They raised money. They made sure everyone ate. They took the parents out to eat and let them laugh, cry and be angry. That is how they built the barn around this family. "We, their friends, all know the rains and the wind will come, and they will be cold—oh, God, will they be cold. But then we will come too…and so there will always be shelter."[4]

During the times we suffer, when we must build those barns around one another, we really experience heaven. There will be no sickness, tragedy or death in heaven, but this is community. This is heaven: Being shelter to one another, sharing joys, feeling welcome, never being lonely. There will be celebrations, the cooking of big meals to share, hanging out and "wasting" time together. Maybe, as Billy Graham has often said over the years, we will build new worlds together. We humans like to do things; we like being productive. But most of all, we will be together doing it, none of us alone, stressed out, frustrated.

We should start practicing, shouldn't we? This is something to look forward to, something we want to be good at by the time we get to heaven. Where do we start if we are living isolationist, Western lives and our days are filled with work and obligations?

Let's begin strengthening our ties with the Body of Christ by working on the relationships God has already given us. Most of us are letting relationships wither through neglect. Everyone is busy working, going to school, doing sports, volunteering. Friends are too busy to meet for a meal or take a walk together. Neighbors hardly know one another. Coworkers are anxious to get home, so they never think of hanging out after work. No one wants to go to the trouble of entertaining at home. We are tired, the house is a mess, and it's a lot of work.

Community simply means being open and spontaneous. Being with others gives us energy. We can invite people over and ask everyone to bring something. We can shove all the clutter into a closet or spare room and close the door. Our guests will not care—their houses look the same!

What defines communal, heavenly-minded people? We must

admit we need one another. We must remember we are part of a Body. We must recognize our culture's isolationism is neither normal nor healthy. We should look carefully at those God has already given us as our community and keep those relationships vital. When we take community seriously, we will not only be able to envision heaven, we will experience it.

ACTIVITIES

1. Begin a new awareness of your heavenly family by getting a piece of paper and drawing three concentric circles on it. Each of these circles represents a level of friendship or relationship in your life.

2. Write the names of everyone in your life with whom you have a relationship and place them wherever they belong. The people with whom you have the closest relationships belong in the innermost circle. In the middle circle go the people you are close to, but they are not soulmates or in your confidence about the deeper aspects of your lives. These are the good friends and close family members, but not the closest friends. In the outer circle are neighbors, coworkers and family members with whom you have more than a casual relationship, but who do not belong in the inner circles. These people are important to you, too.

3. When you are finished placing people in their respective circles, you will have a better idea of community. Is there anyone in your life who has drifted out of your life through neglect? Can the relationship be reinstated and moved closer to the center? Plan some action steps: Call, make a date for lunch or go for a walk together. If the person is homebound or in a nursing home, visit them. You may need to write letters and get back in touch. If you cared enough about someone to put them in your relationship circles, you care enough to do the work necessary to nurture the relationship.

Here are some things you might want to think about when creating your relationship circles:

- How many people have you listed in each of your relationship circles? How are your relationships with these people? Are you keeping in touch, especially with those in the two inner circles? Is there someone in any circle you feel badly about losing touch with?
- How about your spouse, children and other close family members? Could you do more to be available to them, to spend more quality time together?
- Do you know your neighbors? When was the last time you got together with them?

. . • . .

NOTES

[1] Sarah A. Lanier, *Foreign to Familiar: A Guide to Understanding Hot- and Cold-Climate Cultures* (Hagerstown, Md.: McDougal, 2000), p. 60.

[2] Lanier, p. 60.

[3] Lanier, p. 60.

[4] Anne Lamott, *Traveling Mercies: Some Thoughts on Faith* (New York: Anchor Books, 1999), pp. 153–154.

CHAPTER NINETEEN

CREATIVITY

Creativity is God energy flowing through us, shaped by us,
like light flowing through a crystal prism. When we are clear
about who we are and what we are doing, the energy flows
freely and we experience no strain.
—Julia Cameron, *The Artist's Way*[1]

The news was bad, very bad. A coworker's brother had been
diagnosed with cancer and had begun chemotherapy. But something had gone wrong. He was in the hospital, obviously dying.
The atmosphere around the office was somber. Our coworker,
obviously distraught, told us the news and jumped into his car
for the long ride to be at his brother's side.

Some of us began discussing the pros and cons of
chemotherapy. One woman said if she were diagnosed with
cancer, she would wait before allowing her doctors to begin
treating her. "I have some things I want to do. Then I would
come back and let them do whatever they wanted." Curious,

I asked her what she would do. Her eyes got dreamy as she talked about going to Hawaii and writing a book she has been thinking of writing for years. "Why aren't you doing those things now?" I asked. She stared at me for a moment and laughed. "You have a point," she said.

Why do we defer our dreams and put off our creative urges? Are we really too busy? Does it take a terrible diagnosis or a tragedy to wake us up?

A lot of my activities over the last few decades were a means to an end. I really wanted to write, to inspire others, to lead them closer to God. But I could never get "done" with all the other things I thought I had to do. I had children to raise, a house to clean, dinners to cook, errands to run. I volunteered at church and at the children's school. I got a job at a Catholic newspaper, but that was assigned writing, a good experience, but not what I longed to do. What I wanted to do was write books about spirituality. I felt called to that, but my creative side waited and waited for expression. I felt everything else had to be done first. By the time I was done with all those other obligations, there was no time or energy to be creative.

The Creator lives inside each of us; we are the image and likeness of the One who made us. Each of us has a holy, expressive spark, which is meant to be a light within and a reflection of God's light to others. This is our inheritance, our true vocation, to create and prove we are the Creator's children. One of the reasons we are here in this world is to create. Maybe it's the most important reason.

Creativity may be expressed in painting, music, dance, acting, writing, even crafts, but it is not limited to the arts. Creativity includes solving problems, figuring out how things work, parenting, *any* relationship, making decisions, managing money or managing a home. A creative person may work in a corporation, be a stay-at-home mother or be retired. Think of how creative we are when we write a résumé!

Creativity is described in the book of Genesis when God formed the universe. Creativity brings order out of chaos, it makes that which did not exist come into being. "Let there be light" (Genesis 1:3).

We cannot create on the scale God does. We cannot create light or matter or universes. But God gives us the privilege to imitate the gift of creativity on our own, small level. A painter labors to bring something out on canvas only she sees inside her. A composer writes down for our enjoyment the music only he can hear. A writer struggles with the right words to express what she knows to be truth. All are creating something out of nothing, bringing order to what was unformed. Even the dancer, musician or crafter who follows a pattern created by another is creating his own interpretation of the pattern.

We may believe we have never created anything, that we are not "artistic." But creativity follows us wherever we go. We are always creating, whether we realize it or not. Every encounter with another human being, every problem solved, every decision made is an exercise in creativity, a "yes" to the Creator and our own inner spark.

One of the most astounding ways God honors us is by giving us free will. This means, in a sense, we create ourselves. That is how much God respects us. God gives us the raw materials, offers guidance and strength, gives us talents and the desire to use them. There are many roads each of us could take, most of them perfectly fine with God. Each decision makes us a different person. God delights in our good decisions, especially those which create good, new things in the world: a book, a piece of art, a loved child, a happy workplace.

If we have given up on or have never understood our creativity, now is the time to rediscover it. Creativity is not something we do when we are finished with our work: It *is* our work. It is not something we get to do when we retire or when we have enough money to pursue it. Our duties may take up many hours, but we can do them creatively. We may not have traditional artistic talents, but we have gifts. God does not send anyone into this world without an armful of them.

Even if we feel tired, we know that doing something creative, something only we can do, will give us energy. Creativity invigorates us because it is our destiny. We all know people who pursue hobbies, remodel their houses, act in community theater, or sing in choirs during their "off-duty" hours after working all day. We may ask where they get the energy. Being creative gives us enormous amounts of energy that carries over into our jobs and other duties.

We need to honor our inner creative selves. Our creativity is the mark of God, the Creator, in us. Ignoring our creativity is the same as the man in the parable of the talents (Matthew 25:14–30) who buried what the master had given him and brought it back to him unused when the master returned.

From now on let us celebrate our creativity, our God image. At the end of each day, let's ask ourselves, "What have I created today?" Think of more than traditional areas of creativity. Remember conversations, problems solved, meals cooked, repairs made, even prayers said. All are creative endeavors, all need our particular spark and talent to get done. We should give ourselves credit for our creativity and encourage ourselves to be creative in every aspect of life.

ACTIVITY

List at least ten simple things you could do now that would release more creativity in your life. Here are some ideas:

- Redo one corner of a room to be useful, uncluttered and pleasing to you. This could be your reading corner, a workshop, your side of the bedroom.
- Paint a small piece of furniture.
- Fill a new photo album with some theme: a vacation, pets, kids, grandkids.
- Write a letter by hand.
- Repot a plant or plant something in your yard.
- Make soup—or anything homemade.
- Gather your favorite books and find a place for them near your bed.
- Go through your children's old school papers and photos and have a good laugh. Congratulate yourself on what a good, creative parent you have been.
- Go through your clothes. Get rid of anything you aren't wearing, but pull out those special things that really express you and give them a place of honor in your closet.
- Plan a party at your home.
- Plan an outing with some friends you seldom see.

NOTE
[1] Cameron, p. 163.

CONCLUSION

A few days before finishing this book, I went back up the trail where Kelsey and I were lost last year. The "Y" where the neighborhood trail met the main trail had been cleaned up. Someone had cut back all the shaggy bushes and placed a large, flat rock at the trailhead to mark it. What a difference when someone cleared away the clutter.

I hope this book helps you clear the clutter out of your life and grow closer to God. If it helps trim some of the obstacles in your life that keep you from Home, I will be happy. It's no fun to wander around in confusion, stumbling over piles of debris, working long hours and carrying heavy burdens of worry and nonforgiveness. I did that for many years. Many of you are doing the same. It's time we learned a new way to live—God's way.

Where do we start? My friend, Mary, asked me that when I first told her about this book. I shared my own journey with her. I started by allowing myself to relax. I have always loved to read, but when I was in college, I never read anything I liked. My journey began by going to bed a half-hour earlier and curling up with a loved book. I started by rereading all seven of C.S. Lewis's *The Chronicles of Narnia.*

Soon after that, I started keeping the Sabbath. This gave me even more time to read favorite books. After I graduated from college in 2003, I began clearing out my clutter and organizing my papers.

So Mary began a similar journey to clear the clutter from her life. She realized she was "working" every day of the week. Mary is a single mother and visiting nurse with two children, a dog and a cat. She volunteered at her church's nursery on Sundays, often missing the service. Mary was giving and giving to others but never taking care of herself. She left the church she was attending and found another church family where she could relax and be herself and where she could be fed spiritually.

As you work through the lessons in this book, go slowly. Remember the forty years the Hebrew people spent in the wilderness and the forty days Jesus spent fasting. Forty is a Biblical number that means "a long enough time to bring about a real change." Give yourself at least forty days to learn each new lesson. Don't try to do too much at a time or move too quickly. Be patient with yourself. God is.

Don't become discouraged if you revert to your old ways or forget things. Keep working toward the goal. Things will become easier. God will help you. Just ask.

Our lives today can be incredibly confusing and chaotic. Our culture does not help us, but our faith does. God wants so much more for us. God does not want us to settle, to work hard all our lives and then die, to merely be "doers" who forget who we are.

Where should you start? Trust yourself to know that. You know what jumped out at you as you were reading this book.

Don't do the thing you "should" do; do the thing you really want to do.

Your choice just might ignite a new love affair with time and with God.

. . • . .

I would love to hear from readers about how this book has helped you and your stories of clearing out your own clutter. You can contact me through my Web site at www.makeroomforgod.com or by writing to P.O. Box 4198, Apache Junction, AZ 85278.

BIBLIOGRAPHY

Allen, David. *Getting Things Done: The Art of Stress-Free Productivity*. New York: Penguin, 2001.

Anderson, T. Alexander. *The Gift of Time: Making the Most of Your Time and Your Life*. Edina, Minn.: TMPress, Inc., 2001.

Atchity, Kenneth. *A Writer's Time: A Guide to the Creative Process from Vision through Revision*. New York: Norton, 1986.

Brown, Montague. *The One-Minute Philosopher: Quick Answers to Help You Banish Confusion, Resolve Controversies, and Explain Yourself Better To Others*. Manchester, N.H.: Sophia Institute, 2001.

Cameron, Julia. *The Artist's Way: A Spiritual Path to Higher Creativity*. New York: Putnam, 1992.

Chambers, Oswald. *My Utmost For His Highest*. New York: Dodd, Mead & Company, 1935.

Covey, Stephen R. *The Seven Habits of Highly Effective People: Restoring the Character Ethic*. New York: Fireside, 1989.

de Gibergues, Emmanuel. *Keep It Simple: The Busy Catholic's Guide to Growing Closer to God*. Manchester, N.H.: Sophia Institute, 2000.

Greeley, Andrew M. *When Life Hurts: Healing Themes From the Gospels*. Chicago: Thomas More, 1988.

Heschel, Abraham Joshua. *The Sabbath*. New York: Farrar, Straus and Giroux, 1951.

Klauser, Henriette Anne. *Write It Down, Make It Happen: Knowing What You Want—And Getting It!* New York: Fireside, 2000.

Lamott, Anne. *Traveling Mercies: Some Thoughts on Faith*. New York: Anchor Books, 1999.

Lanier, Sarah A. *Foreign To Familiar: A Guide to Understanding Hot- and Cold-Climate Cultures*. Hagerstown, Md.: McDougal, 2000.

Lewis, C.S. *The Screwtape Letters*. San Francisco: HarperSanFrancisco, 1942.

Lewis, C.S. *Mere Christianity*. New York: Macmillan, 1943.

Linamen, Karen Scalf. *Just Hand Over the Chocolate and No One Will Get Hurt*. Grand Rapids, Mich.: Fleming H. Revell, 1999.

Marshall, Catherine. *Adventures in Prayer*. New York: Ballantine, 1975.

Svoboda, Melannie. *Rummaging for God: Seeking the Holy in Every Nook and Cranny*. Mystic, Conn.: Twenty-Third, 1999.

Thibodeaux, Mark E. *God, I Have Issues: 50 Ways to Pray No Matter How You Feel*. Cincinnati: St. Anthony Messenger Press, 2005.

Trepp, Leo. *A History of the Jewish Experience: Eternal Faith, Eternal People*, rev. ed. West Orange, N.J.: Behrman House, Inc., 1973.